# MAGGIE GREENO

A historical narrative on the unusual
life, adventures and achievements of
Margaret Ann (Wallace) Greeno,
a California pioneer woman.

by

George McDow, Jr.

ISBN 0-938373-15-3

First Edition
Design and printing by
Heidelberg Graphics, Chico, Ca.

Distributed by
Lahontan Images, 206 S. Pine Street
Susanville, Ca. 96130
Phone  916 257-6747
Fax  916 251-4801

# CONTENTS

# PREFACE

Early historians and biographers gave only slight recognition to the acts and accomplishments of the pioneer women who stood beside or in the shadows behind their husbands, often providing the ideas, incentive, initiative and encouragement that ultimately led to success.

Margaret Ann (Wallace) Greeno was such a woman—a Boston-born Yankee of strong will and character. Her unique life in the early history of the American west was filled with hardships, excitement, adventure, joy, sorrow and financial reward.

This historical narrative is the product of ten years researching and compiling her lifetime activities—an interesting, fascinating and sometimes frustrating endeavor. The intent of the author has been to write an accurate chronicle of the life of that enterprising and gracious lady, and of the locales in which she resided.

All dates, places and events mentioned herein have been thoroughly researched and rechecked. All persons mentioned by proper names were actual persons with whom she associated, or in some way their actions affected her remarkable and unusual life.

# CHAPTER I

## BOSTON, MASSACHUSETTS

Spring was in the air, a profusion of wildflowers were in full bloom in the meadows and on the dunhills around Boston. Before sunrise on June 3, 1838, Elizabeth Anne Wallace awakened from her slumber, uncertain what had aroused her. A vague wave of uneasiness washed over her as she lay listening to the hoofs of the milkman's horses clattering on the cobblestones of Boston's narrow winding streets, as he made his early morning deliveries to the multistory, red brick row houses.

Suddenly a wrenching pain in her abdomen brought her to the realization that the child in her womb was signaling it would soon make an appearance. When the pain subsided, she changed her position and closed her eyes briefly before reaching over to wake Thomas.

Thomas, in the excitable manner inherited from his French ancestry, dressed quickly and, after making sure Elizabeth would be all right for a short time, sped to his mother-in-law's flat a few blocks away. In a matter of minutes he was hammering on the door of the Collins' residence off Ann Street, frantically calling her name. The upstairs window swung open and the nightcapped head of mother Collins appeared. She inquired in a slightly Scottish brogue if Elizabeth was all right. Thomas informed her the pains had started. She told him to return to Elizabeth, and she would follow immediately.

Elizabeth, in spite of repeated spasms, was in complete control when Thomas returned. She told him to bring clean towels and sheets, and to start a fire in the coal stove in the kitchen so water could be heated.

Thomas had the coal fire burning and was filling the kettles when Mother Collins arrived. She went directly into the bedroom throwing back the sheets she ran her hands over Elizabeth's enlarged abdomen to determine that movement had indeed started. She took stock of supplies Thomas had laid out. Satisfied, she joined him in the kitchen where she selected the wash basins she'd need, informing Thomas as to what order he was to bring them to her.

In a few hours Mother Collins was holding the small healthy baby girl in her hands. As she carefully sponged the infant off with warm water, she thoroughly inspected it for any defects, and finding none she wrapped it in a blanket and laid it in the new crib, handcrafted by Thomas.

Workaday sounds of creaking wagon wheels on the cobblestone streets, with their cargoes on the way to the docks, reminded Thomas that it was past the hour he should be getting to his carpenter job. He had forewarned his employer that his wife was expecting, and that he might be late, or called home at any time. Assuring himself that Elizabeth and the baby were all right, and that Mother Collins would look after them, Thomas reluctantly departed for his day's work.

It was late afternoon when Thomas returned to their small flat. Mother Collins had prepared their evening meal, and while they ate she listed the duties he'd need to perform during the night.

After Elizabeth was rested and was provided a light evening meal while nursing the baby, the question of a name for the child came up for discussion. Elizabeth wanted to name her Ann after her mother, but Thomas opted for Margaret, after his mother. Mother Collins, a diplomatic lady, settled the question by suggesting both names, Margaret Ann. It was agreed upon, and the name Margaret Ann was duly inscribed in the Bible. She was to be called Margaret, but in later years it would be shortened to Maggie.

Mother Collins went back to her flat leaving the young father with her promise to return early the next morning before he had to leave for work.

That night held many new experiences for Thomas. Each time baby Margaret Ann fussed, he picked her up. Sometimes it was only a diaper that needed changing; other times it was hunger, and he gently placed her in the arms of Elizabeth for feeding. He was overwhelmed with a new sense of love and devotion. A new and wonderful dimension had been added to their lives, and he was keenly aware that an unrealized vacancy had been filled. The happy father sat very still as he contemplated the joys and happiness that lay ahead for his small family.

During the following year, the proud parents shared the joy of watching Margaret Ann grow and begin to observe the world around her. They rejoiced in helping her take her first step, hearing her first words, and watched her auburn hair develop into beautiful curly locks. With great pride they took her on their Sunday walks to view the many brigantines, schooners, and barks tied up at the wharves taking on cargoes bound for England, the Caribbean and other seaports. Sometimes they would walk up Beacon Hill, admiring the expensive homes belonging to Boston's elite. Thomas would point out the homes he had made repairs or alterations on, describing in great detail the fine furniture and art objects he had observed. Other times they enjoyed strolling on the Commons, visiting with families picnicking under the shade trees. Often they walked along the waterfront until they reached the dunhills of South Boston, climbing to the crests where they sat on the warm sand. While eating their picnic lunch, they watched the billowing sails of the vessels making their way in or out of Boston Harbor.

Severe New England winters kept the family confined to their small flat, venturing out only for an occasional visit to Grandmother Collins or Grandmother Wallace. Snow often clogged Boston's narrow streets and sidewalks, and horse-drawn sleighs became the only means of transportation. Large chunks of ice in the harbor slowed shipping. Many captains and ship owners found cargoes in southern ports for shipment to warmer climes. Those who could not sought refuge at anchor in well-protected coves among the many capes of Boston Bay. The warehouses along the wharves filled with cargo, waiting the arrival of spring.

Thomas Wallace found the winter months a difficult and exhausting time. Regular construction and alteration work slowed. Winter storms never ceased to find leaks in roofs, requiring immediate attention under the most harsh and difficult conditions. Working in the inclement weather often sent him to his bed with chills and fever. Elizabeth, his loving wife, prepared hot broths and applied mustard plasters to relieve his congestion.

In the late fall of 1840, while nursing Thomas through an early bout with the grippe, Elizabeth began to experience morning sickness, and it was soon evident that she was again pregnant.

In June of 1841, after Margaret's three birthday candles had been blown out, the cake cut and sampled and her presents unwrapped, played with and put away for the night, Elizabeth attempted to explain to her that she would soon have a baby brother or sister; but with her birthday gifts fresh in her mind, she was unimpressed with the coming event.

A few weeks later Elizabeth was again awakened with abdominal pains. The delivery went almost as before. This time Thomas set up little Margaret with her play things in another part of the flat, so that she would not interfere with Mother Collins. In due time a baby boy made his appearance. Elizabeth insisted they name him Thomas, for his father, and his birth was recorded in the family Bible. When Thomas took Margaret into Elizabeth's bedroom to see her new brother she was filled with awe. The rag doll she had gotten at Christmas lost much of its appeal.

The new baby caused many changes in the family's routine. Elizabeth was unable to give as much attention to little Margaret, however, Thomas made a special effort, when he was at home, to give her as much attention as possible. It soon became evident they would be needing a larger flat with more bedrooms. There being no vacancy in their building, they began checking other buildings along Congress Street. In October 1842, they found a flat suitable to their needs. They moved the block and a half to a four-story red brick row house near the Hay Market. At four-and-a-half years, Margaret was caught up in the excitement of the move, and of having her own bedroom decorated with bright spring flowered wallpaper and window curtains that accented the motif.

Old enough to enjoy the yule decorations, Christmas that year was exciting for Margaret. When on Christmas Eve the carolers sang in the snow covered street in front of the building, she was enchanted. On Christmas morning she was delighted with the bright red sled Thomas had built and painted for her. She could hardly contain her excitement that afternoon when Thomas took her to a nearby street where other neighbor children were coasting.

The family's spring and summer Sunday walks and picnics again became less frequent in 1843, as Elizabeth had again become heavy with child.

On August 1, 1843, William H. Wallace, named for his Grandfather Collins, made his appearance. The crib Margaret and Tommy had outgrown was resurrected, and the baby blankets were again put to use. Grandmother Collins took Margaret and Tommy home with her to spend the nights until Elizabeth was able to resume her normal duties.

In the fall Margaret entered nursery school during the afternoons, a new and exciting experience for her. It was the first time she was among a group of boys and girls her own age. She was quick to pick up the routine and soon made new friends. Before Margaret realized it, winter and foul weather had again descended upon Boston.

Christmas was a joyous time that Margaret looked forward to with great anticipation. Tommy did not comprehend the excitement displayed by Margaret, but was most impressed with the ball and wooden blocks he found waiting for him on Christmas morning. The children's interest in the spirit of Christmas intensified when they heard the sound of carolers' voices in the street and when Grandfather and Grandmother Collins arrived, for the family Christmas dinner.

As the spring thaw opened the north Atlantic shipping lanes, the activities on the docks increased. Tommy watched the horsedrawn traffic on the street from the window during the day, while waiting Margaret's return from school.

Thomas' hours away from the flat increased as his carpenter skills became more in demand in the fast growing city of Boston. Only on Sunday was the family able to enjoy their familiar walks and picnics on the south Boston dunhills, on the Commons or along the waterfront. They never ceased to marvel at the vast number of sailing ships discharging cargoes of spices, silks and exotic artifacts from the Orient, or taking on cargoes of leather goods, molasses, lumber and cotton goods for Europe.

By 1845, Boston had become an important port for the trans-shipment of goods from the Orient, South America and the Caribbean to ports in Europe. The outbreak of war between Mexico and the United States added to the demand for sailing vessels to carry military cargoes of guns, caps, gunpowder, shoes, uniforms, blankets, tents, saddles and harness to the gulf coast ports to supply United States forces. Ship captains and owners were expending every effort to increase the speed tonnage capacity of their ships. Boston's shipyards were beehives of activity, extending or adding masts on the schooners and barks in order to spread more canvas to the winds and increase their speed.

The shipping enterprise of Howland and Aspenwall, Boston's largest shipping company, contracted with shipbuilder John Griffith to design and build the fastest ship he could conceive. The result of his effort was the *Rainbow*, the first China Clipper. It started its first run on February 1, 1845, and Captain John Lamb proclaimed that "the ship could not be built to beat her."

Thomas was fascinated by the quality of craftsmanship going into building those new ships, and he marveled at their sleek designs. When the opportunity allowed he steered his family walks in the direction of the shipyards to observe the progress being made on the new sailing vessels.

During the week Thomas was kept busy remodeling old three-and four-story brick buildings in the northeast section of Boston, converting some of them from flats into rooming and boarding houses to accommodate the ever-increasing number of seamen required to man the hundreds of sailing ships calling Boston "home port."

Most of the talk in the mariners houses, on the docks and about the city concerned the Mexican War. Each returning ship that dropped anchor in Boston harbor brought tales, picked up in Gulf Ports, about the progress of the United States' forces against Santa Anna's army.

Margaret, now seven, was learning a great deal about Mexico and the southwestern territory, as her schoolmaster utilized the war news in his geography teaching. He pointed out various localities making news, and the vast areas of the North American continent to the west, as yet unsettled by white people. During the week Margaret's attention was taken up with her homework, but she found a few hours on weekends to play with her new school friends.

The holiday season with its accompanying winter snows made coasting the enjoyable winter sport for children. Thomas, during his slack period, spent time with Margaret and Tommy on the slopes. He added to their sledding pleasure by pulling them back up the hill after they coasted down.

When school resumed in January 1846, Margaret was happy to again be among her young friends. The teachings she received from the strict schoolmasters did much to stimulate her desire for more knowledge. The fascinating stories of strange sights and places the seamen related to her father impressed her as she began to search out and read books and papers on various subjects about the world.

Time rolled by. Margaret was nine in 1847, when word was received in Boston that an armistice had been signed, ending the war with Mexico. Discussions around the Wallace dinner table began to center on the reports Thomas brought home about all the wonderful opportunities for settlers in Texas, now that it was United States territory.

Thomas, like many others, began to talk about the advantages of going west, and getting some of that good land that was free for the taking. On occasions Elizabeth had to bring him back to the realization that he had a wife and family to support, and the children needed the education that Boston's schools provided. Furthermore, she reminded him, he had no experience farming or stock raising.

Margaret was fascinated with the stories her father told of that wonderful land, and her imagination often ran wild with thoughts of exciting adventures that might unfold living in that great western land.

By early 1848, the cargoes of arms and army supplies passing through Boston's harbor had given way to cargoes of clothes, leather goods, canned and salted fish, molasses and household necessities to supply the settlers moving into the newly acquired Texas and California territories. Ship captains had waiting lists of people seeking passage to the new territories.

Activity increased along the docks in mid-summer 1848, when ships from China, by way of the West Coast and Mexico, brought word of the discovery of gold in California. At first people were skeptical, but the ships' captains confirmed the reports that the miners were in desperate need of mining tools, clothing, food stuffs and whiskey.

In the fall, ships returning from California had many shanghaied crew members that replaced the original sailors who had jumped ship in California. They spread stories in the seamen's boarding houses of the successful gold seekers who had bags of gold nuggets sluiced from the streams.

The sea captains docking that fall were anxious to unload their cargoes of hides and take on new shipments of mining equipment, tough boots and other commodities for the western miners, before winter closed the harbor. Adventurous men began begging the captains for passage on the long voyage around Cape Horn to California.

By spring of 1849, the discovery of gold was the main topic of news coverage in the Boston Herald and other New England newspapers. The rush to the golden west began in full force. Some Bostonians had taken off overland on foot or horseback, or by whatever means of transportation they could find, hoping to join parties in Iowa and Missouri organizing to travel overland by ox-drawn wagon trains. Others were trying to book passage on the ships sailing to California, or by the more hazardous sea/land route to Panama or Nicaragua. There they would take a chance on crossing the isthmus on foot or by native pack burros, and catching a ship on the Pacific coast going north to California.

Thomas was caught up in the excitement. it was hard for him to control his urge to join the Argonauts and start for the West Coast, especially when William Hall—the young carpenter he had spent the last five years training—decided to go to California and try his luck in the gold fields. Bill Hall almost persuaded Thomas to join him, relating stories he had heard of the great demand for carpenters in the mining camps and new towns springing up. He was convinced that if he couldn't find gold, he could still make a living as a carpenter.

Each time Thomas broached the idea of trying his luck in California, Elizabeth reminded him that he had a family to support, and that it would be more prudent to take advantage of the good wages available in Boston. She further argued that they should accumulate a nest egg before making a move to a far away place with an uncertain future. Although Elizabeth confessed to herself that the idea of going to that new and exciting country did appeal to her, with a young family in school, the thought of moving was impossible.

Margaret celebrated her twelfth birthday on June 3, 1850. Elizabeth prepared a picnic and invited the girls in her class to join them on the Commons for games and refreshments. The bevy of young girls soon attracted the attention of several boys playing ball nearby. They joined the girls and Elizabeth stretched the provisions so that each uninvited guest received a sample of birthday cake.

Stories the sailors told of the gold strikes in California continued to fire Thomas' interest. When another carpenter friend, M.G. Kellog, informed Thomas that he and his seamstress wife Louise, a good friend of Elizabeth's, had decided to sail to California and try their luck in the mining camps, Thomas again broached the subject to his wife. She admired Louise's daring, but again cooled Thomas' ardor for the wild west.

During the winter of 1850-1851, Boston experienced the heaviest snowfall known to that time. Blocking sidewalks and streets, it closed down the horse-drawn rail cars throughout the city. An avalanche of snow slid off the roof of Park Street Church, catching a number of pedestrians on the sidewalk by surprise. Getting the children to school became impossible; Margaret, Tommy and Billy were house bound until the storm subsided.

Over-exertion from shoveling snow off walks and leaking roofs caused Thomas to suffer his usual winter cold and fever. This year the symptoms did not pass with Elizabeth's ministration of hot broths. The congestion in his chest was not relieved by the mustard plasters, and his fever continued to climb. Elizabeth summoned the doctor, who administered every medicine that he knew to clear the congestion in his chest. Nothing seemed to work, and Thomas became weaker and weaker. Finally the inevitable happened. Thomas's heart could no longer get the oxygen needed from his lungs and he gradually passed into unconsciousness as life left his suffering body.

Elizabeth was devastated. She blamed herself for not going to California's warmer climate, as Thomas had often proposed. It took several weeks for her and the children to adjust to the fact that they no longer had Thomas to depend upon for support.

# CHAPTER II

## MOSES OAKES

Moses Oakes, Sr. was among the first of Thomas' friends to call on Elizabeth after learning of his death. Moses offered his sympathy, and volunteered to help in any way he could. Following the funeral, Moses again stopped by the flat and renewed his offer of help. Having lost his wife of many years, he understood the shock and grief that had been thrust upon Elizabeth and her children.

Several local housewrights offered to take over Thomas' business, but they did not want to adequately compensate Elizabeth. She sought Moses' help, and he was able to arrange a sale for her that paid a fair price for the tools and stock in trade, giving her a small sum of cash. Thomas had a small insurance policy but it was obvious that she needed to find a regular source of income to support her family.

Moses Oakes, who operated a boarding house for seamen, was having his problems with cooks and housekeepers. He suggested to Elizabeth that she consider taking the job of housekeeper and cook at his place. He offered to pay her a good wage, and hire another woman to assist her. Margaret, a well-developed twelve and a half year old girl, could help wait on the tables during the evening meal, for which he would pay her a small stipend. The family could take their meals there, relieving Elizabeth of food costs.

At first she was dubious of her ability to plan and

prepare meals for fifteen or twenty hungry seamen. Moses convinced her that he was good at the planning, and knew the amount of food that was necessary to be prepared. He would continue to do the purchasing, and would help out with his boys when needed.

Elizabeth, having no better prospects in view, agreed to take on what appeared to be an overwhelming task. Margaret was happy that Moses had offered her the chance to help the family by assisting in serving the rough and rugged seafaring men who stayed at the boarding house when their ships were in port.

Elizabeth soon realized that the distance from their commodious flat on Federal Street was too distant from the Ann Street boarding house, and a less expensive place to live would have to be found. She and Margaret spent their free time. searching for a less costly flat within a reasonable walking distance from Oakes' boarding house.

A high tide on April 14, 1951, accompanied by heavy rain, hail, and snow submerged the low areas of Boston before they could find anything suitable. Water stood three feet deep on the central and long wharves. The Charles and Mystic Rivers overflowed their banks and rafts had to be improvised for use on some Boston streets. Elizabeth was forced to pick a circuitous route along high ground to get from her flat to the boarding house. Meals were late that day, because Moses Oakes had a difficult time getting to the market to find provisions.

The storm turned out to be a benefit to Elizabeth. Some tenants living in the lower elevations of the city, fearing a recurrence of high water, began to vacate their flats. A vacancy at number 11 Grove Street prompted Elizabeth to move her family there. The small flat would not accommodate all the furniture and household utensils collected in fifteen years of married life.

Elizabeth found a second hand dealer who bought the surplus items, paying her a few cents on the dollar of their original cost. The new flat was used only as sleeping quarters; the family spent the day at Oakes boarding house, except when the children were at school.

Margaret, nearly thirteen, was in her last year of primary school. Tommy, now ten, was in the fifth grade and William, whom the seamen called "Billy," was eight years of age and in the third grade. Moses Oakes' oldest boy, Moses Jr. was sixteen years of age and out of school. He had a laborer's job on the wharf at the Howland and Aspenwall warehouse, and had high hopes of getting a job aboard one of the sailing ships as a deckhand, and working his way up to a full fledged seaman. John Oakes, his brother, was thirteen and in his last year of school.

Elizabeth put up lunches in used lard pails for all the children. During the school week none of the children were around the boarding house from after breakfast until after school. On Saturday and Sunday, Margaret would make breakfast and lunch at the flat for herself and her brothers, clean the flat and do the family laundry.

On weekends, the three Wallace children would go to the Oakes' boarding house for their evening meal. Margaret would help with the serving, and after clearing the tables the two families and the other hired hand gathered around a large table for their evening meal. This provided the opportunity for the families to become well acquainted. On occasions, Margaret and John Oakes assisted each other with homework, but it was usually Moses Jr. who seemed more than willing to help Margaret.

Late in the fall of 1851, Elizabeth received a letter from Louise Kellog informing her that they had arrived in California safely after a rough voyage around Cape

Horn. After spending some time working in Yerba Buena (San Francisco), they moved to a mining town called Forbestown in Butte County. Her husband had been kept busy at his carpenter trade, and had not yet done any searching for gold. She had been swamped altering and repairing clothes for the miners and merchants. There were only a few other married women in the town who had accompanied their husbands. However, there were a number of prostitutes of various races. They had found the housing conditions bad and the price of food and supplies high, but they had been making a good living and enjoyed the mild climate. She asked Elizabeth to write and tell her about things in Boston.

Elizabeth immediately dispatched a letter telling Louise about the hard winter in Boston, and of Thomas' death. She added that, "he might still be alive if we, too, had moved to California."

Several changes took place in 1852, affecting the lives of both the Oakes and the Wallace families. Moses' lease expired on the building at 283 Ann Street, forcing him to search for another location. After some frantic searching he found a building at 171 Ann Street. He was able to negotiate a satisfactory lease, and with some minor alterations it made a suitable boarding house. Moving all the beds, tables, chairs, kitchen equipment and providing services to his tenants at the same time required the assistance of two dray companies. Even with the help of several extra people it was a very busy, long and tiring day.

Among the faces at the Oakes' table in 1852 was a tall thirty-eight-year-old Massachusetts native named Josiah West. He had spent the last twenty years sailing the seven seas. Now, approaching middle age, he was seriously considering abandoning the life of a seaman and settling down to a more mundane occupation ashore. He was, however, hesitant to resign his seaman job with Howland and Aspenwall until he secured a business connection on land.

The Wallace children and John Oakes were fascinated by the tales Josiah told of the distant lands he had visited, and the strange people he had seen. Moses Jr. found Josiah's suggestions on ways to get a job aboard ship to be good sensible advice. He asked many questions of Josiah regarding life at sea and the duties and problems an inexperienced seaman could expect to encounter.

When her duties allowed, Elizabeth listened with interest to the dialogue Josiah West had with the children and other residents. She was impressed by his polite manners that seemed a little out of place for a twenty-year veteran of the seas, and with the rugged good looks of this man her own age.

Josiah also seemed to be impressed by Elizabeth. After learning she was a widow, and mother of the children who seemed to have taken a liking to him, he began to take advantage of every opportunity to visit with her. As the days passed they became friendly, and he confided to her that he was tired of the sea life—it no longer held the excitement it one time had. He was beginning to feel that he was missing something in life that could never be found at sea.

When the day came for Josiah's ship to sail, Elizabeth and the children were saddened to see him leave. He assured everyone that the voyage would end in a few months and he would be back. Tommy and Billy walked with him to the dock, and waved to him as he ran up the plank returning their wave.

During the next few months everyone at the Oakes' house seemed to miss the jovial presence of Josiah. The children missed his cheerful dialogue, and the young seamen missed his valuable advice.

Margaret's fourteenth birthday passed on June 3, 1852. Two weeks later she graduated near the head of her class, and bid farewell to her schoolmaster and classmates. Moses Sr. immediately added to Margaret's duties at the seaman's house, assigning her chambermaid duties in the rooms on one floor and she still waited on tables at meal time. The additional wage she received was a big help to Elizabeth. Margaret was now able to buy personal items such as shoes and cloth for her dresses and aprons, and contribute to the rent. Tommy, nearing twelve years, was also picking up a few odd jobs enabling him to help clothe himself, and have some spending money for an occasional stick of candy.

Everyone was delighted when Josiah West returned from his long voyage to China and California. He brought news of both successful and disappointed gold seekers bargaining for passage back to the East Coast. The successful ones offered to pay for their passage with gold nuggets. The unsuccessful ones offered to work aboard ship for their passage home.

Josiah seemed especially pleased to get back and find Elizabeth still working at the Oakes' house. He brought both Elizabeth and Margaret small gifts from the Orient. Josiah began to ardently seek the companionship of Elizabeth, whenever she could spare the time away from her duties in the kitchen and laundry. In their conversations relative to Josiah's desire to become a land-lubber, Elizabeth suggested that operating a boarding house for seamen was an idea. She mentioned that Moses was continually turning away prospective boarders because he had no room for them. She had also heard that other seamen's houses were crowded and were turning away men looking for room and board while in port.

Josiah began discreetly talking with Moses about the pros and cons of operating a seamen's boarding house. He quickly learned that there were many problems involved. One had to be extremely careful about taking in boarders who quickly drank up all their wages. One also had to beware of those inclined to frequent gambling houses where they were soon relieved of their pokes, not leaving anything to pay their board bill. Moses required his tenants to pay weekly in advance, in order not to be left holding the bag when they shipped out. There was always a problem finding competent kitchen help. Moses expressed himself as being fortunate to have Elizabeth heading up his kitchen and her daughter Margaret to help in the dining room and with housework.

It was only a matter of a few weeks before Josiah's ship had been unloaded and reloaded with cargo for California, the rigging all checked and repaired, the canvas restitched and the galley stocked with food for the long voyage around the Horn. He reluctantly reported to the ship for what he told "Anne"—as he had started calling Elizabeth—that was to definitely be his last voyage.

It was late fall when Josiah again arrived back in Boston. After being dismissed by the ship's captain, he headed straight for the office of Howland and Aspenwall. There he informed them that he appreciated sailing for them those many years, but that the time had come for him to put down roots on land, and that he would not be making any more voyages.

At the Oakes' boarding house he broke the news to Elizabeth Anne that he was back in Boston to stay. He informed her that he was considering opening a seamen's boarding house, providing she would join him in operating the house, and also would consider becoming his wife. Anne was surprised at Josiah's proposal. Although she had developed a warm feeling for him, she also felt an obligation to Moses for having provided her with badly needed employment after Thomas' death.

Anne had been breaking in, and teaching her helper Nancy Malander, a twenty-eight year old Boston native, to handle the kitchen chores, just in case she or one of the children should become ill. Moses had encouraged Nancy's progress, realizing the possibility of unforeseen circumstances that might cause Anne to be indisposed. She had noted that Moses seemed to be somewhat smitten with Nancy, as he was always willing to bestow small favors upon her.

Anne had also begun to notice that young Moses Jr. had started to notice Margaret's full curvaceous figure, her long auburn hair and her big sparkling blue eyes. He was casting, what Anne thought was a lustful eye toward Margaret as she moved about serving the young seamen.

She told Josiah about her feelings of loyalty and gratitude toward Moses, and her concern that the seamen and Moses Jr. were becoming a bit too familiar with Margaret. Josiah confided he also had a long friendly acquaintance with Moses Sr., and would not want to cause any animosity between Oakes and her or himself. They finally decided to meet with Moses, and truthfully lay their problem on the table. They would state they were seriously considering marriage, and Josiah was also considering opening a boarding house, as he had observed Moses continually turned away prospective boarders. Should they marry, Anne would be leaving her duties at Oakes to participate in operating their boarding house.

When they met with Moses, Anne pointed out that Nancy Malander was becoming well versed in the duties that she had been performing, and with some additional help could take over. Moses was not as disturbed about their plan to compete with him as they had expected. He did, however, express some surprise and re-gret that Anne would be leaving. He requested that she stay on during the coming holiday season, and help train an assistant for Nancy. He also indicated his plea-sure that Anne had found a good reliable companion to help her raise her boys, as he thought they needed the guidance of a father figure. Moses even offered to host a wedding reception for the couple following their cer-emony.

Having made agreeable arrangements with Moses, Anne then set about tactfully gaining the approval of Margaret, Tommy, and Billy. Margaret professed some reservations about leaving Oakes; however, Tommy and Billy were both greatly impressed with Josiah, so it took very little persuasion to win their approval.

In the meantime, Josiah set out to find a building with a suitable kitchen, dining room, parlor, and bed-rooms that would accommodate fifteen or twenty boarders. He finally found a three story red brick build-ing at 346 North Street, just a couple of blocks from the house that once belonged to that famous rebel and sil-versmith, Paul Revere. He leased the building in Janu-ary 1853, and bought the beds, linens, and other furni-ture from the former tenant at a reasonable price.

As the holiday season drew to a close, Elizabeth Anne Wallace and Josiah West recited their marriage vows in front of the Reverend Father Peter Kroes, in the presence of Anne's family, Moses Oakes, his boys, and Nancy Malander. Following the wedding ceremony, the newlyweds were heartily toasted by all the seamen at the Oakes' boarding house.

Anne gave up her flat on Grove Street, and with her children moved to Josiah's house. It was not long before she and Josiah, with the help of Margaret and Tommy and even ten-year-old Billy, had the building ready to receive boarders. Moses referred several seamen he was unable to accommodate to Josiah. When word spread along the docks that Josiah had opened a boarding house, seamen of all ages who had sailed with him, or met him in ports around the world, began to search him out when they were in Boston. It was only a matter of a few months before he too was having to turn them away.

With Josiah, Anne, and Margaret working full time, and Tommy and Billy helping after school, the family was able to handle the work for the first few months. When additional help was needed they employed Ellen McGerry, a seventeen-year-old colleen from Ireland.

A frightening experience for the family occurred on April 14, 1853. A fire broke out only a few blocks away in the Washington and State Street area. Gunpowder stored in one of the houses exploded, scattering the fire over a wide area. Three children were killed in the fire that completely destroyed eight houses. After the flames eventually burned themselves out, the city of Boston passed regulations requiring all inhabitants to provide themselves with long ladders that would reach the ridge of their houses, and twelve-foot poles with a large swab at the end to damp out sparks that might land on the roof.

Josiah immediately complied with the new regulation, acquiring the necessary ladder and pole. He acknowledged that he hoped he never had to climb the ladder three stories to the ridge to damp out sparks.

Margaret's move to Josiah's house did not end Moses Jr.'s attention to her. If anything, his visits to the West's boarding house became more frequent. At first, he came only on Sunday afternoon, but by mid-summer, he was showing up three evenings a week. They strolled along the waterfront, or watched the neighborhood ball games. When traveling entertainers scheduled a show in Boston, the two of them were usually in the audience for at least one performance.

In the fall, Moses Jr. informed Margaret that Howland and Aspenwall had promised him that in the spring he could go to sea aboard one of their new clipper ships. He would have to begin as a deckhand, but the seaman's wage would be more than he'd received as a dockhand. Margaret had become accustomed to Moses' companionship and admitted she would be lonesome while he was away.

At the McKay shipyard, Margaret and Moses watched as the new vessels received the final rigging and canvas. They watched with interest when McKay's *Great Republic* was launched and were impressed with the majestic sight of the ship as the sails unfurled for the shakedown cruise. There was speculation between them as to which of the new clippers Moses would sail on. Margaret could understand the pride and exhilaration a seaman would experience as a crew member of such a magnificent vessel.

As winter days grew shorter and nights longer, Moses spent nearly every evening with Margaret. They could be found sitting in the dining room, by the light of a single flickering taper, holding hands and whispering as young lovers are wont to do. An occasional snicker or giggle punctuated their conversation.

The lease on Moses Oakes' boarding house was due to expire on December 31, and his landlord was asking an unreasonable increase to renew. Moses Jr. noticed a "to let" sign on the building at 358 North Street, one block from Josiah's place. Moses Sr. made a deal with the owner, and moved his establishment to the new address on the first of January 1854.

Shortly after they completed their move, young Moses was informed by Howland and Aspenwall he would be assigned to a clipper ship scheduled to sail on

February 15, to the southern United States ports to pick up a cargo of cotton.

The security of receiving steady seaman's pay prompted Moses to pressure Margaret into an early marriage, even though he would be gone for some time. She agreed, and after informing their parents of their decision, they called on Father Peter Kroes at his parish house at 118 Endicott Street and made arrangements for the wedding.

At high noon, February 13, 1854, the young couple repeated their wedding vows in the presence of Josiah West, who gave the bride away, her mother Anne, and her brothers Tommy and Billy, Moses' father and brother John. Friends who attended were Ellen McGerry, Joseph and Margaret Reynolds, and their son James. The Reynolds occupied a flat on the third floor of the Oakes's boarding house.

After the ceremony, they repaired to Wests' boarding house for the wedding feast. The young couple were toasted with fine French champagne provided by Moses Oakes, Sr.

Urged by Josiah and Anne, Margaret decided to remain in the Wests' home, and continue her duties assisting in the operation of the boarding house. Moses moved his personal belongings to Margaret's room, as he expected to be away for extended periods of time, with relative short layovers in home port.

Moses went to sea on his first voyage as scheduled and Margaret busied herself at the boarding house. Tommy and Billy, who Josiah had accepted as his own sons, were beginning to be known by the name of West.

Moses returned from his first voyage to Charleston and Savannah in about two months. He brought Margaret and Anne presents he had picked up in Charleston. The time passed quickly for the newlyweds and it was only a few days before his ship's cargo was unloaded and reloaded for the next voyage. When Moses reported to the ship, Margaret walked with him to the wharf. She stood watching and waving good-bye as Moses walked up the plank and stepped over the gunwale, to disappear from her view among the canvas and rigging. Standing alone, Margaret began to sense the feeling of loneliness she was destined to endure as the wife of a seafaring man. With a tear in her eye she turned and slowly retraced her steps to the boarding house. Moses did not make it back to Boston by June 3, 1854, when Margaret reached her sixteenth birthday. Anne, Tommy and Billy had. not forgotten the day. Anne prepared a nice birthday cake, and Tommy presented her with a small gift. Josiah wished her many happy birthdays and tried to keep her spirits high, because he realized she missed Moses not being there to help celebrate the occasion.

# CHAPTER III

## THE BABIES

Margaret had joyous news for Moses Jr. when he finally made a late summer return to Boston. She had been experiencing morning sickness and had put on a little weight. The additional weight was immediately noticed by Moses, so he was not overly surprised when she confided to him that she was pregnant. her uncertainty about his reaction to her condition was relieved when he expressed his great delight in becoming a father.

In a short time, Moses was back at sea, and Margaret was experiencing the discomforts of an expectant mother. It was late in the fall of 1854, when Moses arrived back in Boston. Margaret and Anne were both busy sewing baby clothes, and Josiah West was searching the stores for a crib.

At Josiah's insistence, Margaret had consulted a doctor who assured her that both she and the baby were in good condition, and that she could expect a normal birth, probably around the Christmas holidays. Moses was delighted to learn of all the preparations and the doctors report. His only concern was that he would be at sea during the birth of his child.

Moses fears held true. The vessel he served aboard was scheduled to the southern climes during the winter months, making port calls in the Caribbean, Brazil and Argentina before rounding the horn into the Pacific with a final destination of California.

The Christmas season at West's boarding house was a festive occasion, with the expected arrival of Margaret's baby at any time. The crib and the blankets were ready, as were the tiny garments Margaret and Anne had sewn during the fall. Christmas Eve and Christmas day passed with the exchange of gifts, and a sumptuous New England dinner was enjoyed by all, including the boarders.

It was early in the evening on New Year's Eve when Margaret first began to experience sharp pains. They were coming far apart but when she mentioned them, Anne insisted she lie down and start timing their frequency. It was early morning January 1, 1855, when Margaret's pains began to increase in frequency and intensity. Anne sent Tommy to the doctor's house with the message that Margaret was going into labor, and asked that he come soon as possible. The doctor followed Tommy back to the boarding house, and in due time, with Anne's assistance he delivered a baby girl, whom Margaret named Jane Minerva Oakes.

When Moses returned early in February 1855, not only did he have a new daughter awaiting him, but another unexpected development had taken place during the months he had been at sea. His father Moses Oakes, Sr., forty-three years of age, and his cook and housekeeper Nancy D. Malander, thirty years of age, had decided that they were in love and would get married.

On February 18, 1855, Moses L. Oakes, Sr. and Nancy D. Malander, in the presence of Moses Jr. and Margaret, Josiah and Anne West, Joseph and Margaret Reynolds, John Oakes, Tommy, and Billy West, were joined in holy matrimony by the Reverend Father Peter Kroes. Following the wedding ceremony Josiah and Anne West hosted a reception for the newlywed couple, where they were amply toasted by the happy group of well wishers.

Moses Jr. had very little time to get acquainted with his baby daughter. The vast migration of people to the West had created a heavy demand at California ports for all types of materials manufactured in the New England states. The ship to which Moses had been assigned was soon loaded with a cargo of clothing, boots, molasses, dried fish. and whiskey. It was scheduled to pick up sugar and spices in the West Indies to replace the depleted stocks of California merchants.

William H. Aspenwall, Gardnier Howland and Henry Chauncey had taken over the United States Postal contract to carry mail by steamship from, New York to Chagres on the east coast of Panama, and from Panama City on the west coast to Astoria, Oregon. They had built five steamships to ply the waters between New York and Chagres twice a month, docking at Charleston, Savannah, New Orleans and Havana, going and coming. Three steamers were required on the Pacific side.

Many old time seamen were dubious about sailing on the new-fangled, steam-powered paddlewheel vessels. Several steamers in experimental voyages had experienced boiler explosions and fire aboard, and in some instances the ship and crew had been lost. There were arguments among the seamen at the boarding houses as to the practicability of steam-powered vessels. The fact that the sleek new clipper ships were still able to sail faster than the steamers strengthened the arguments of the older sailors. Moses, like most of the younger sailors, was quite impressed with the steam-powered vessels. Had Aspenwall and Howland's steamers been sailing from Boston, he would have readily accepted a job aboard one. Their regular schedule would have let him get back to Margaret and baby Jane, on a more frequent basis.

Shortly after Margaret's seventeenth birthday on

June 3, 1855, Moses returned to Boston and the arms of his loved ones. He spent his short time in port getting acquainted with his six-month-old daughter, cuddling her in his arms during the day. The nights he spent making love to his wife. The days in port passed rapidly. Before the lovers realized it, the time came for Moses to report for another long voyage to California with the usual cargo of supplies for the gold seekers.

Margaret was again feeling lonesome, but her duties assisting Anne with the housekeeping and the added responsibility of caring for little Jane, helped keep her mind off her longing for Moses. About six weeks after Moses had sailed, Margaret became certain that she was again pregnant. As the fall season descended on Boston, morning sickness and the usual discomforts of expectant motherhood began to occupy her thoughts and actions. She had to curtail her more physical activities such as bed making, furniture moving, and running up and down the many stairs in the boarding house.

The holiday season passed, and Margaret had gotten quite large around the waist. Jane had her first birthday, and Moses Oakes Sr. again lost his lease on the North Street house. He located another building down the street and around the corner at number 4 Clark Street. He readily made the move and was soon back in business.

When Moses Jr. returned, he was surprised at all the changes that had taken place since his last sailing. Little Jane, a year old, was beginning to pull herself up and to stand alone. His father had moved to a new address, and Margaret was well into her eighth month of pregnancy with their second child.

His clipper ship was put in dry dock for repairs and to have the barnacles scrapped and the bottom retarred, a process necessary to improve the ship's speed.

He was grateful to have the extra time ashore out of the rugged North Atlantic winter weather, and especially thankful to be at home when Margaret gave birth to their first son on February 12, 1856. They named him, Thomas, in honor of her father and brother. Moses was so delighted to have a healthy son that the name was of little consequence to him.

Things were just beginning to get settled back to normal around the Wests' boarding house, following the arrival of the new baby, when Moses was called back to his ship for another California sailing. The winter of 1856 had been exceedingly rigorous in New England and the storms showed no signs of letting up. Moses was somewhat apprehensive about sailing out of Boston in such cold and stormy weather. His concern was lessened with the knowledge they would be heading south into the warmer climes of the southern hemisphere. There, the duties on board, such as handling the canvas and climbing the rigging, could be accomplished under milder and smoother conditions.

It was an unusually cold and stormy winter. Keeping the warming fires stocked with coal, shoveling snow from the roof and sidewalk, and repairing leaks around the windows took its toll on Josiah West. He had on occasions become overheated, exhausted, and soaking wet, only to become thoroughly chilled by the freezing arctic winds blowing in off the Atlantic. He was plagued with a cold. Anne's mustard plasters, hot broths, and an occasional shot of hot rum did little to relieve his discomfort. The doctor's visits and medicines had no effect on the congestion in his lungs, and Josiah's once powerful physique became weak and emaciated. After weeks of suffering, death claimed his soul, and his body was laid to rest in the Copps Hill burial ground.

Anne and Margaret, although broken hearted by the loss of the man they loved and relied upon, vowed to keep the boarding house operating, at least until Moses returned and could participate in their decisions. They found it extremely difficult operating the boarding house without a dominant male in charge to subdue the fiery tempers of some of the more belligerent boarders. Tommy, who was sixteen, helped with the heavier work, but he was no match for the cantankerous old salts. Billy, thirteen, helped after school and tended the babies during the busy supper hour.

Anne somehow found time to write her friend Louise Kellog in California, telling her of Josiah's death and of their efforts and frustrations in operating the boarding house.

In mid-July 1857, when Moses ship arrived back in Boston, the homecoming was not as joyous as had been anticipated. Somewhere in the tropics, on the return voyage, he picked up a tropical fever. The captain and first mate administered all the remedies they had aboard, but were unable to subdue the fever. Moses had to be helped ashore in Boston, and was taken by carriage to the boarding house. The Captain advised Margaret to keep him isolated until advised by a doctor that his condition was not contagious.

Margaret immediately summoned the doctor who, after checking his condition and the information the Captain had supplied, concluded that Moses had contracted some form of malaria that had severely weakened his body. The doctor said it was important that he be kept isolated, and that everything he came in contact with be thoroughly sterilized in boiling water. Those attending him should immediately wash and scrub their hands and face upon leaving the room. Moses Sr. was kept informed of his son's condition. He and Moses' brother John were permitted to enter his room to give him encouragement. The fever failed to respond to any of the medicine. Within two weeks his condition deteriorated, and death followed quickly. He was laid to rest beside Josiah in the Copps Hill burial ground.

Margaret at nineteen, heart broken and overcome with grief, was now in the same situation as her mother: a widow with two small children to support. Money from Moses' small insurance policy would not last long, even with the most prudent of expenditures, and she knew she would somehow have to rise above her grief and take charge of her life. In the meantime, the two women continued to keep the boarding house operating.

Not long after the tragedy, Anne received another letter from her friend Louise Kellog, extending her sympathy on the death of Josiah. They had moved from Forbestown to a mining camp called Inskip. It was high in the hills above the west branch of the Feather River where a Dutchman with the name of Enskeep had found gold. Her husband, although not a miner, had acquired an interest in a mining claim by grubstaking a prospector. He kept busy building houses in the rapidly growing town, and Louise's talent as a seamstress was very much in demand by the miners and merchants. She also mentioned there was great demand for women to work in the hotel kitchens and dining rooms.

Anne answered Louise's letter, thanking her for her consolation and for the information about the new town of Inskip and the possibilities for work there. She also advised Louise of their latest sorrow in Moses' passing.

The letter from Louise gave Anne and Margaret something different to think about. They began to discuss their options in a more realistic way. They quizzed the seamen who had been in California ports about information they may have learned regarding life in the mining camps, and what opportunities might be open to women.

Margaret and Anne discussed at length the pros and cons of moving to California. The boarding house was becoming more burdensome and Tom, approaching seventeen, had been talking about going to sea, which would leave them short-handed. The deliberation began to favor a change of environment, and the West Coast to look more attractive. Tom thought California would have more opportunities for him than going to sea, and fourteen-year-old Bill saw it as a great adventure and was ready to go.

They finally decided to give up the lease on the North Street house, sell the furniture, and go to California. Moses Oakes Sr. disliked the thought of his grandchildren moving so far away. In all probability he'd never see them again, but he had to agree they would be better off than to stay in Boston and endure the severe New England winters.

As widows of Howland and Aspenwall seamen, Margaret took it upon herself to talk with a representative of the company about passage to California on one of their ships. He agreed to provide cabins on their U.S. mail steamship from New York to Colon, Panama, then on their Pacific mail steamship from Panama City to San Francisco, at a discounted rate for her and Anne, Tom and Bill at half rate, and the small children would be free of charge. They would be obliged to provide their own transportation to New York, and to pay the rail fare across the isthmus on the newly constructed Panama railroad.

The promise of discounted fares solidified their decision to make the major move. Anne notified the landlord they would not renew the lease the first of the year, and she wanted to sell the furniture, linens, and the kitchen and dining room utensils. She told him that if he leased the house to another person for a boarding house she would offer that person a deal on all the equipment.

As the holiday season drew near, Anne began notifying the boarders the house would close on the last day of December. The landlord brought by a prospective tenant who was interested in continuing the operation and in purchasing the furniture, utensils and supplies. Among the three of them, they worked out a mutually satisfactory deal. Anne agreed to stay with the new owner for thirty days and help break in his staff.

On Jane's third birthday, January 1, 1858, the family moved into a small flat where they remained until spring. In February, after Anne had fulfilled her obligation at the boarding house, she found time to write a letter to her friend Louise. She informed her that she, Margaret, and their children would be leaving Boston in March or April on their way to California to join them. Uncertain as to when they would reach California, Anne suggested Louise send a letter in care of the San Francisco postmaster explaining where and how to find them. She would pick the letter up when they arrived in San Francisco.

At the Boston and Maine Railroad station, the air was charged with emotion that spring day in 1858, as the two widows prepared to leave their native city: pretty nineteen-year-old Margaret Ann (Wallace) Oakes with her two small children, and forty-four-year-old Elizabeth Anne West with her two teenage sons.

Tears flowed freely as they kissed their friends good-bye. Moses Oakes hugged and kissed his two grandchildren, and helped them board the train as the conductor shouted "All aboard."

The train ride was a new, strange, an exciting experience for all. The steam locomotive pulled its short train of cars westward, through Massachusetts farm country where they saw, scattered on the rolling hills, well-kept farm houses and out-buildings. After a stop at Worchester, the country became more hilly until the tracks broke out into the Connecticut River Valley near Springfield. The train stopped there for water, passengers and mail. When they crossed the Connecticut River, the valley soon gave way to the Berkshere hills. Margaret and Anne wondered if the mountains in California were anything like the Berksheres. Late in the afternoon, the train moved out of the hills into the Hudson River Valley in New York State, arriving at Albany about sundown. It had been a long day for the traveling family. They immediately hired a hack and were driven to a hotel for overnight lodging.

After a warm meal in the hotel dining room, they retired. A strange city, a strange hotel and a strange bed were at first frightening to Margaret, but she was exhausted from, the long journey and soon fell into a sound sleep, wedged between her two small children.

They were awakened the next morning by a loud banging on the door, with a wake-up call announcing that breakfast would be served within the hour.

Margaret hurriedly dressed and got the children ready. After packing their night clothes in her carpet bag, Margaret and her children descended the stairs to the lobby where Anne and her boys were waiting.

When breakfast was over they checked out of the hotel, and Anne hailed a hack to drive them to the New York Central Railroad station.

Aboard the New York Central train they began the second leg of their journey. After an enjoyable ride through the beautiful Hudson River Valley, they arrived in New York City. Margaret hired a transfer wagon to haul their trunks to the Atlantic and Pacific Company's dock at the end of Warner Street on the North River. There they checked them through to San Francisco. A public carriage took them to a small hotel, recommended by Howland and Aspenwall, near the wharf.

In all probability, they would never visit New York City again, so they made the most of the extra day before sailing by hiring a Hackman to drive them around Manhattan Island, and show them the major points of interest.

On sailing day, following a leisurely breakfast, they checked out of the hotel with their small bags, containing clothes and toiletries they'd need aboard ship. They took a hack the short distance to the wharf where the steamship was berthed. She was a beautiful, side-wheel steam-powered vessel; her fore and aft masts were rigged with square and schooner sails to conserve on coal.

When they were settled in the small adjoining cabins that would be their home for the next several days, Margaret and Anne were paid a visit by the ship's captain. He expressed his sympathy for the loss of their husbands, and explained the ship's schedule and route. He promised to see them safely aboard the new Panama Railroad at Colon for the trip across the Isthmus to Panama City. He assured them the Panama Railroad had the most modern and commodious passenger cars, and that on their arrival in Panama City they would be embarked, free of expense, on the Railroad Company's steam tug that would take them to the Pacific steamship awaiting at anchor in the harbor.

At 2:00 o'clock, promptly as scheduled, the steam whistle blew and the big side-wheels started turning. The ship started moving slowly away from the dock, and out into the waters of the Hudson River. With smoke belching from the stack, the ship picked up speed. The deck became crowded with New England passengers, as well as with many from New York getting their last look at the Manhattan skyline.

# CHAPTER IV

## "PETE" KELLY

The first evening at sea, after they had finished supper, Anne and her two sons excused themselves, anxious to go on deck and watch the sunset, while Margaret stayed with her children. The day had been hard on Jane, who was starting to doze in her chair, and Thomas still dawdled over his food.

The good-looking, well-dressed young man that Margaret had noticed casting glances her way on deck that afternoon was sitting at a table nearby. He came over and, speaking with a slight Irish brogue, introduced himself as Charles R. Kelly, adding that his friends called him "Pete." He offered to help Thomas out of the high chair, and to carry Jane, who by that time was drugged with sleep.

When they reached Margaret's cabin, she thanked him for his help, and explained that the children were exhausted by the long trip from Boston. Pete Kelly bid her good-night, and said he was glad to have been of assistance to her and should she need further help with the children while on the voyage, he would be pleased to oblige.

The motion of the ship reminded her of a time she and Moses had sailed on Boston Bay in a small craft, before Jane's birth. With other memories of her old life passing through her mind she gradually dropped off into a sound sleep.

As the days passed, Margaret and Pete Kelly became

better acquainted. He began to share the same table at mealtime with the two ladies and their children. He told them that he was raised in New York, and had worked at a variety of jobs none of which he found interesting, but he had managed to save enough money to pay for passage to California, where he was sure his fortune lay in the gold fields. He had assumed the two ladies were on their way to join their husbands in California, and upon learning that Margaret was a widow, his interest in her became more intense.

During the voyage through the Caribbean Sea, with the tropic air sweeping over the deck billowing the helper sails, Margaret, Tom, and Bill spent considerable time on deck, enjoying the warm refreshing breezes blowing through their hair. Anne preferred the cabin and willingly attended her grandchildren.

By the time the paddle-wheeler tied up at the wharf in Colon, on the Atlantic coast of Panama, all but the babies had the beginnings of a healthy suntan, from the tropical sun. When the ship was securely docked and the gangplank in place, the captain, true to his word, sent a couple of deckhands to assist Margaret and Anne carry their luggage to the Panama Railroad. They found Pete Kelly waiting at the gangplank to offer his assistance with the children. Margaret graciously accepted his offer, and he carried Jane aboard and helped locate their seats in the brightly colored passenger car.

After the passengers' luggage and the United States mail was stowed aboard the baggage car, the steam locomotive and its gaily painted string of cars began its three hour, forty-seven and a half mile run through the lush Panama jungle, over the most expensive railroad line ever built Margaret, with her little group of travelers—now including Pete Kelly—watched with great interest and amusement as the locomotive's whistle frightened the monkeys and multi-colored jungle birds, scattering them to the treetops along the way.

The train for the first part of the trip, followed along the Rio Chagres. Until four years before, this river had been used by Panama natives to ferry thou-

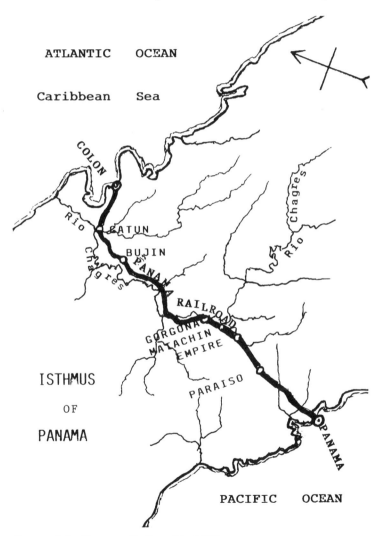

Route of the Panama Railroad in 1858.

sands of gold seekers three quarters of the distance across Panama by canoe. The wayfarers, loaded down with their rifles pistols, bowie knives, picks, shovels, and bedrolls, endured the blinding heat, torrential rains, swarms of mosquitoes, and epidemics of dysentery. They were forced to finish their trek on foot or by muleback to the Pacific coast, where, with luck, they could find a sailing ship headed for California.

Highballing along, the locomotive slowed only at the villages of Gatun and Bujin, allowing donkeys and cattle to clear the tracks. When the train stopped at Gorgona to take on boiler water, vendors with exotic jungle fruits and handcrafted wares met the train, hoping to entice a few U.S. coins from the passengers. Margaret and Anne watched with interest from the window, while Pete, Tom and Bill left the train to purchase a bunch of bananas and look over the offerings of the native peddlers. Jumping aboard the train as the departure whistle blew, they returned to their seats to share the bananas with their companions.

The native villages of Matachin, Empire and Pariso, were passed with only a blast of the locomotive whistle and a slight slowing of speed. A little over three hours after the passengers boarded the train at Colon, the locomotive and its string of bright colored cars pulled into Panama on the Pacific coast. While waiting their turn to board the steam tug that would take them to the steamship at anchor in the bay, Margaret and the others passengers were able to observe some of the local color. The thatched huts and native dress proved interesting, although the occasional lack of the latter caused some shock and embarrassment to the Puritan-bred New England widows.

Assisted by Pete Kelly and native porters in boarding the tug and then the steamship, Margaret and Anne settled into their cabins for the final leg of their long journey to the wilds of California. Six days later, the steamship put into port at Acapulco, Mexico to take on fresh provisions and mail. Declining the invitation of Pete and other passengers to go ashore, Margaret and Anne observed the activities of the Mexican port from the deck of the ship. Margaret thought it best not to expose the children to possible disease that might be prevalent on shore. When its stores were resupplied, the ship continued its voyage north, along the coast of Mexico. Shortly after rounding the Cape of Baja, everyone aboard was pleasantly entertained by a pod of whales on their annual migration to the northern Arctic waters. The whales seemed unconcerned about the steamship and swam nearby for two days.

The last day at sea, Margaret rose early to pack her bags and to observe the shoreline of the new state of California, the place they would soon be calling "home." She watched the grass-covered hills along the coast as the steamer chugged north a few miles off shore. Finally, the ship changed course to enter the Golden Gate. The two families joined most of the other passengers on deck as the ship passed through the narrow strait into the smooth waters of the bay. A wild cheer went up from the passengers as the first houses on the San Francisco hills came into view.

The bay was full of ships. Some of them had been abandoned eight or nine years earlier during the peak of the Gold Rush; others were in use as ferry boats carrying passengers and cargo across the bay to other settlements. Sailing ships used in the coastal and China trade could be seen loading commodities for their return voyages.

Margaret and Anne found the fast-growing town of San Francisco alive with activity. Pete hailed a carriage to take them to the Sansome Street House, recommended by Aspenwall and Howland. As they entered the lobby to register, Margaret took notice of a "Help Wanted" sign in the window. She inquired of the desk clerk and was advised they wanted people with chambermaid and dining room experience. Pete inquired about the need for male help, and was told to talk with the house saloon keeper.

Settled in their rooms, Margaret bathed herself and the children, and changed all of them into fresh clothing. Anne, Tom, and Bill walked to the post office, where Anne found a letter from Louise Kellog waiting for her. Back in the Sansome Street House lobby, Anne opened the letter in which Louise expressed her joy in learning that they were going to join them.

Louise explained how it would be necessary for them to take the riverboat up the Sacramento River to Sacramento. From, there they would have to ride the Wells Fargo Stage to Oroville, and then come to Inskip by mule train, or possibly find someone with a light wagon or buggy that could navigate the narrow winding pack trail through Pence's ranch and up the ridge between the west branch of the Feather River and Butte Creek. They would pass through the mining camp of Dogtown and the Lovelock and Powell ranches before reaching the new mining camp of Inskip. Margaret and Anne were amazed to learn that the really rugged part of their trip lay ahead of them.

In the Sansome Street House dining room that evening, Margaret, Anne and the children were again joined by Pete. He had been making inquiries about getting to the gold fields, and had learned that the greatest need for miners was in the area of the Stanislaus River. The town of Columbia had sprung up there following the discovery of gold along the banks and gravel bars. The town had burned to the ground the previous year, and was now in the midst of a rebuilding boom. Getting to Columbia, he had learned, was relatively simple. One had only to take the San Joaquin River boat to the town of Stockton; from there, stages ran directly to Columbia and other mining towns.

Pete told Margaret his meager funds were nearly depleted, and that he had been offered a job as bartender in the Sansome Street House Saloon. This would let him save enough money to move on to Columbia, or maybe Inskip, in a few months.

Pete also made it known to Margaret that he had become very fond of her and the children. He asked her to consider marrying him. Although only a few months had lapsed since the passing of Moses, Pete suggested that given the present circumstances, and Margaret's responsibilities of caring for the children, she would not be out of line with generally accepted practices to consider matrimony. He pointed out that they could conserve finances by renting a flat or housekeeping rooms in San Francisco. He could work at the saloon rebuilding his stake to support them in the mining camp until he could make a strike or get into some business endeavor.

Margaret, although somewhat attracted to Pete, had not intended to become seriously involved with another man until the usual period of mourning had elapsed. Pete's discussion of finances was a disturbing subject, one to which she had not given much thought. Having been the wife of a regular paid seaman, finances during her married life had not been a problem. The modest insurance left her had been adequate to cover her current traveling and living expenses. Now she was suddenly aware those funds would soon become exhausted and she would have to find a means to replenish them.

Surprised by Pete's unexpected proposal, uncertain of her true feelings for the handsome gentlemen who had been so kind to them during the voyage from New

York, and not wishing to reject him outright, she told him she would need time to consider his offer before making such a serious decision. Back in her room after the children had been tucked in bed, Margaret sat by the flickering glow of the kerosene lamp and contemplated the surprising proposal. The following morning she confided in Anne the attraction she felt toward Pete, and the reservations she had about becoming involved so soon after Moses' death. She also discussed the idea of remaining in San Francisco for a period of time to sort out her feelings.

Later that morning when Pete met Margaret in the lobby, he told her he'd decided to take the saloon job until he could get something better, or accumulate enough money to pay for passage to the gold fields. The subject of the proposal didn't come up, but she told him that she was considering looking for a flat or housekeeping rooms in San Francisco until she could resolve many questions in her mind about her future.

Anne had no reason to remain in San Francisco. Her original destination had been the mining town of Inskip, in Butte County, where the Kellogs had assured her she could make a living operating a boarding house or doing laundry for the miners. The high cost of hotel rooms and meals in San Francisco set her to immediately arrange for transportation. She booked passage for herself and her two boys on the river boat to Sacramento, and Wells Fargo stagecoach on to Oroville. From there she took a chance on finding some means of transportation up the ridge to Inskip.

Margaret's search for housing in San Francisco was not easy, with a three-year-old girl and a two-year-old boy. Margaret found the landlords looked with skepticism on a young widow's ability to meet rent payments and support small children. Two or three landlords were brazen enough to accuse her of desiring a place to engage in prostitution.

After several days of searching, Margaret finally located housekeeping rooms in a big house owned by a matronly widow, whose sons had answered the call of the Gold Rush and were seeking their fortunes somewhere in the Sierra Nevada. To avoid the harsh storms in the mountains, they returned to San Francisco and spent the winter with their mother.

In order to conserve her funds, Margaret arranged with the landlady to act as a nanny for the children during the day and early evenings, while she took employment waiting on tables in the dining room of the Sansome Street House.

On days when their shifts coincided, Pete would walk Margaret home and play with the children. At the same time he made every effort to convince her to consent to his proposal, using the argument that one set of housing would be to their mutual advantage. At that time , he was living in a rooming house where breakfast was provided. It was only a few blocks from Margaret's rooms. He called on her often, and accompanied her and the children on walks about the city, observing the sights. He also told her stories of gold strikes he heard at the saloon.

In winter, some miners temporarily deserted their diggins along the streams and sought more comfortable accommodations in the city to wait out the winter storms. Stories of their finds and their disappointments were the main topic of conversation.

Many idle gold miners were attracted by the pool tables and card games in the saloon. Pete listened with great interest as he tended the wishes of those men with the full pouches of gold dust and nuggets. He asked many questions, trying to find out where a neophyte would have the greatest opportunity to make a strike.

Christmas season in San Francisco in 1858 was vastly different from those Margaret had enjoyed in Boston. The west coast merchants added to the Christmas spirit by hanging evergreen boughs, red paper streamers, and bells in their stores. City residents utilized evergreens and ivy to decorate their doors. Many householders hung a sprig of mistletoe where it might best serve its purpose, while a few of the more well to do residents set up evergreen trees in the bay windows of their homes. The churches made attempts to form caroler groups, but nothing to compare with the well organized and trained groups that had for years contributed to Margaret's holiday spirit back in Boston.

Shortly before the holiday season arrived, the landlady's two sons returned from the gold fields for the winter. Margaret did not see any signs of great financial success. She inquired about the conditions encountered, and the opportunities a person might have to find gold. They confided that very few prospectors had struck rich deposits. Most were barely able to eke out a living along the Sierra streams, but all remained confident that with continued prospecting they would eventually come across a rich deposit. They admitted it was a lot of hard work. Many were suffering from lack of food and shelter, and those who did manage to find a few grains of gold made the saloon keepers and professional gamblers rich.

Armed with this information, Margaret suggested to Pete that maybe he should consider staying in San Francisco and seeking permanent employment. He was more inclined to listen to the tales of rich strikes he heard from the braggarts in the saloon. Their stories whetted his dream of finding his fortune in gold.

By the end of February 1859, most of the prospectors were getting their mining equipment and supplies together and making arrangements to return to their claims and continue their search for that elusive yellow metal. Jane had turned four years old on the first of January, and Thomas turned three on February 12. When Pete showed up with a birthday gift for Thomas, he found the landlady's boys packing for their return to the hills. He asked for their suggestions as to the best area to start looking for gold. They informed him that they were going to the Sonora and Tuolumne River areas: that area around the mining camp of Columbia had produced well last season. Although a devastating fire on August 25,1857, had consumed the greater part of the town of Columbia, most businesses were rebuilding with brick. Carpenters and brick layers were in great demand. If a person was unable to find ground to work, he was sure to find a job as a laborer in town.

They explained to Pete that on occasion, when short of supplies and unable to find sufficient gold-bearing deposits to maintain them, they took work for other claim holders or shopkeepers until they had accumulated another stake to allow them to continue their search. The past season, they worked nearly all summer on the construction of a sixty-mile-long ditch and flume from the Stanislaus River to supply water to the Columbia area, to feed the hydraulic monitors.

The boys' enthusiasm for the prospects around the Columbia area sold Pete. He would have packed up and gone with them, but his infatuation with Margaret kept him from leaving without her.

During the next few weeks, Pete renewed his efforts to persuade Margaret to marry and go with him to Columbia, where he was sure he could make his fortune. He used every beguiling means available to an amorous suitor; finally, Margaret gave in to his proposal. Together they went to the City Hall, procured a marriage license, and, in the chambers of the Justice of the Peace, were united in marriage.

They handed in their resignations the same day, and began making preparations for the move to Columbia. Margaret penned a note to Anne telling her of her marriage and their planned move to Columbia, and advising her mother that she would write and tell her how to communicate with them when they were settled.

The first part of April 1859, found Pete Kelly, his bride, and her two small children on a San Joaquin River boat headed for the town of Stockton. There they took the first Wells Fargo stagecoach on which they could book passage for Columbia. The road from Stockton was a well-used dirt stage road, heavily traveled by all means of transportation. The stage overtook and passed large freight wagons loaded with construction materials for rebuilding the town, and supplies for the merchants' shelves.

On their arrival in Columbia, they found virtually a tent city, with several new brick structures arising from the ashes of the terrible conflagration the town had experienced in August, 1857. The newly completed City Hotel was commanding top prices for its few available rooms. Margaret and Pete had no choice but to pay the outrageous price asked. They immediately set about locating some type of living quarters. After hours of searching, Pete found a disappointed gold seeker with a fairly large tent, and utensils for cooking outdoors over an open fire. He was anxious to sell his equipment for enough money to get back to San Francisco. Without waiting to check with Margaret, Pete tied up the deal with a sizable deposit.

Margaret was not happy with Pete's purchase, although she was convinced he had taken the only option open to them. Pete promised it was just a temporary solution to their housing problem, but Margaret began to question her judgment in letting him talk her into bringing the children to such a godforsaken place.

They were sheltered only by an old canvas tent. She had to cook and heat water over an open fire with smoke and sparks blowing in her face, while fighting off flies and mosquitoes. The outdoor privy consisted of an old canvas stretched around some small poles, between which a deep hole had been dug, and the seat was a board nailed to the poles across the open hole. An indescribable stench permeated the air in all directions.

Pete, who was anxious to get out in the hills along the streams in search of gold, had been obliged to accept work helping carpenters and bricklayers in order to support his newly acquired family. There were jobs available to Margaret, but she had no one to whom she'd trust the care of her children. She was compelled to spend her time in the tent. Their marriage and living conditions in Columbia were not the blissful event two young lovers would normally expect, and Margaret was constantly prodding Pete to find more suitable accommodations.

Following the big fire in Columbia, one of the first actions of the town trustees had been to debar the Chinese people from residing within the corporate limits. Although most of the Chinese miners lived outside the town boundary, there were some that had rather nondescript shacks just inside the town, which had escaped the fire. The Chinese found a ready market for those so-called houses among residents who had lost their dwellings in the fire. Most of those people had, by the summer of 1859, replaced their original dwellings or made other living arrangements. Some of the old Chinese shacks were becoming available for purchase or rent. Pete rented one, and Margaret, anxious to get out of the tent, agreed to move into the dilapidated old shack where there was a separate bedroom. The cooking could

City Hotel (built 1857), Columbia Historical Park. Photo by McDow 1988.

Main Street in Columbia Historical State Park, Tuolumne County, California. Photo by McDow 1988.

be done indoors on a small wood stove that provided heat for the two rooms. She still had to carry water, and the privy was still outdoors, but now, instead of a canvas, there was a wooden structure that enclosed the open pit. When the privy was not in use, a board covered the wooden seat to help keep the obnoxious odors from penetrating the air.

Pete's desire to get out in the hills and locate a deposit of gold got the best of him at times. When a report circulated around Columbia of some prospector making a new find, Pete, like many others, would take off from his job and join the rush to the reported area. He would spend several days searching in the hope of finding a deposit. Being a neophyte and having no knowledge of geology, he was usually lucky if he found any ground that produced over a few flakes of gold. The great demand for carpenters, helpers, and hod carriers was the only reason he was able to get back on a job when he returned from one of his sojourns.

Miners coming into Columbia for supplies often reported their finds as far in the opposite direction, in order to avoid having their discoveries overrun by hordes of gold seekers. That fact did not sink in with Pete or his equally inexperienced prospecting cronies. They stood ready at any moment to take off in pursuit of the yellow siren.

This on-again, off-again employment did not provide the steady income that was needed to pay the rent and put food on the table, let alone build any surplus reserve that would let Margaret even hope to improve their living situation. This led to continual bickering between them. Each time Pete returned, disappointed and broke, he would promise that he would not be led astray by wild rumors again, and that he would stay on the job until they had accumulated enough money to afford a decent house.

An early September rain settled over the California foothills. The creeks ran full. Rumors of new deposits being exposed by the high water proved to be too much for Pete to resist. He took off, with two of his pals, to prospect the streams and ravines in the area. Margaret was fit to be tied. She realized that Pete would never change. The lure of gold was too strong, he would never keep his promises, and there was no way they could possibly live on his unsteady wages.

Margaret in despair, tried to determine what action she could take. Where could she go? What could she do to support herself and children? She was walking down Main Street when she met the two sons of her former San Francisco landlady. They had been driven out of the hills by the unusually heavy storm, and were preparing to leave the area for the winter. Margaret told them of the problems she'd put up with and the ones she feared were to come. The young men expressed their sympathy, and told her they'd seen the effect of the siren's cry of gold had upon many men. The temptress had pulled men, playing upon their greed, from their families, from businesses, even from pulpits and judicial benches, with the wild promise of vast wealth. The boys sensed that Pete had responded to the siren's call, and would never settle down for any length of time. Their suggestion to Margaret was to try and forget about him and consider returning the San Francisco, where she could find work and someone to care for her children. They would be leaving in a few days and offered to let her travel along with them if she wished. They said they would help with the children and her luggage, and even offered to loan her some traveling money if she needed it.

She thanked them for their kindness and said she would think it over and let them know the next day.

Actually, it took only a few hours to make up her

mind. Taking a thoughtful look at her miserable surroundings, she concluded she was not going to subject herself and her children to that type of lifestyle any longer. Six months was enough. She did not wait until morning. That evening she took the children and walked to the American Hotel, where the boys were staying, and told them she had decided to return with them to San Francisco, and would appreciate the help they offered.

That night, by the dim candlelight, Margaret wrote a long letter to her mother at Inskip. She told her of the

Wells Fargo Express building (built 1857), Columbia Historical State Park. Photo by McDow 1988.

many problems and disappointments she had endured with Pete the past six months, and admitted the marriage had been a mistake. She advised Anne that she had decided to accompany her former landlady's boys back to San Francisco, where she would try to seek lodging again with their mother.

The next morning, Margaret went to the D.O. Mills' Bank in Columbia, and drew out the remaining funds she had on deposit from Moses Oakes' insurance policy. She left a small amount in Pete's account, as she knew he would need it when he returned. Then she went to the Wells Fargo office and purchased stage tickets to Stockton. By evening she had their clothes packed and her trunk filled with her few prized personal possessions.

The following morning she walked to Mullian and Williams livery stable where she hired a wagon and driver to haul her trunk to the stage office. She arranged for its shipment to San Francisco.

Margaret left a note with a neighbor to give to Pete. In it she explained she had tried to be brave in the face of adversity, but she could no longer subject her children to the kind of life he offered. She was returning to San Francisco, and would seek a legal separation. Her mind was made up and he need not make any effort to follow, or try to persuade her otherwise.

The stagecoach left Columbia at mid-morning carrying Margaret, with Thomas on her lap and Jane at her side, the two brothers, a clothing drummer, and a camp-following gambler. A disappointed prospector agreed to ride shotgun alongside the driver. The well-paired, four-horse team easily pulled the Concord coach along at a mild gallop, winding through the foothills and over the dusty road in the valley. At Stockton they were forced to lay over a day while the riverboat unloaded its cargo and took on a supply of wood for its boiler.

As the paddlewheeler moved away from its dock and started down the San Joaquin River toward the San Francisco Bay, Margaret cast one last glance east toward the Sierra foothills, heaved a sigh of relief, and promised herself she would never again let a man talk her into a situation such as she had experienced the past summer.

They awoke the following morning just as the riverboat docked at San Francisco. The sight of the city was even more welcome than when she first observed it upon entering the Golden Gate the year before.

Margaret and the children went with the brothers to their mother's house. The landlady was as surprised to see Margaret as she was to see her son's early return from the mountains, and she greeted them all with open arms. Fortunately for Margaret, the rooms they had occupied before had recently been vacated. She was allowed back on the same arrangements as before. Margaret applied and was immediately re-hired at her old job at the Sansome Street House.

Before the week was over, she contacted an attorney and explained the situation experienced at Columbia. He recommended filing for an annulment. She filled out the necessary papers, and the attorney-filed them with the court. After a sufficient time had elapsed, and no response came from Pete, the judge granted Margaret the annulment.

Margaret had begun to experience nausea, and spells of feeling faint, which she attributed to her worry that Pete would contest the court action. She needn't have worried, for he was too afflicted with the gold fever. Nevertheless, she consulted a doctor, who advised her she was three months pregnant.

Pregnancy was a totally unexpected development, She had not considered she might be carrying Pete's child. A new baby would entail problems she hadn't counted on. Trying to make a living and being so far away from friends and family was extremely frightening. In her frustration she wrote a long letter to her mother in Inskip, damning the turn of events and seeking her counsel.

# CHAPTER V

## INSKIP 1880

It was a couple of weeks before Anne's reply reached San Francisco. She advised Margaret to take heart and make the best of the situation. Telling her that she had room in the house she was renting for Margaret and the children, Anne suggested they come to Inskip well before the time for the baby's birth. Anne informed Margaret that she had kept busy doing washing and ironing for the town's single men, as well as for the miners in the area. She mentioned that Tom, now seventeen, was working for a nearby mining operation, and Bill nearly sixteen, was helping feed and care for horses in the livery stable of Mr. Coleman's hotel.

The letter was comforting to Margaret, as she now had someplace to go, and someone to care for the children during her confinement. Margaret dispatched a reply to Anne, expressing her appreciation for the offer of hospitality and assistance. She advised Anne that she wanted to continue working as long as possible, and that sometime before spring they would come to Inskip.

Margaret continued waiting on tables through the holiday season, even though she was becoming large around the waist, and very uncomfortable at times. When she left, the headwaiter complimented her on the job she had done, and told her there would be a job for her anytime she desired to return.

The booming, bustling mining town of Inskip, on the ridge between Chico Creek and the Feather River in

62

Inskip Inn (built 1868), the only remaining commercial building in Inskip, Butte County, California. Photo by McDow 1988.

Butte County's Kimshew township, had become the primary stopover point on the mountain trail. It was used by saddle and pack-trains transporting miners and supplies over the Sierra Nevada mountains into Humbug Valley, Big Meadows, Honey Lake Valley, and on east to mining camps in Idaho and Nevada.

It was early in the spring of 1860. The gold mines along the ridge were flourishing, and the mining excitement along the trail ahead in Nevada and Idaho territories created a back-log of miners and packers with their mule-trains at Inskip. While they waited for the snow pack to melt, these men filled the town's five hastily erected wooden hotels. Many people were camped in tents near the town.

Inskip saloon keepers endeavored to quench the thirst and provide games of chance for the marooned travelers and packers. The saloons thus proved to be very lucrative.

Inskip merchants, who usually transported their own merchandise, called upon some of the stranded packers to store their own cargoes, and to use their mules and horses to bring in additional supplies from Oroville and Marysville.

It was into this environment that Margaret, eight months pregnant with Pete Kelly's child arrived. Her two other children were now four and five.

At Pete Coleman's hotel, the driver stopped to get directions to Anne's house. It was a rough board-and-bat house a short distance up the road. A few minutes later, Anne heard the spring wagon's wheels grate on the gravel, and ran out to greet her daughter and grandchildren. The driver helped Margaret and the children from the wagon, and they fell into each other's arms in a happy reunion.

The luggage was unloaded, and Anne helped the driver move the trunk into the room she had prepared for Margaret. Margaret paid the driver and Anne insisted he partake of some food and drink before starting the return trip. She told him he might get some return fares if he stopped at Downer's and Kelley's hotels on the way out.

Shortly after the driver left the house, Margaret's youngest brother came in from his labors at the Coleman stables. Bill had developed into a husky, good-looking young man. He and Margaret fell into a loving embrace like all siblings who have been parted for some time.

Near nightfall, Margaret's brother Tom arrived from his labors at the mine. He was covered with mud and dirt from the sluicing operation where he was employed. Margaret was so delighted to see him that she embraced dirt and all, placing a loving kiss on his cheek.

While the boys were washing and changing into clean clothes, Anne was busy setting the table and preparing the evening meal. Margaret began to familiarize herself with the new surroundings. She tried to assist but Anne continually admonished her "to sit and rest," reminding her the trip had been long and tiring for one in her condition. Anne promised that tomorrow they would go see Doctor J.S. Carter, so he could assess her condition and so that she could become acquainted with him before she needed his service.

Anne called Jane and Tommy, who had been busy looking into every nook and cranny about the house trying to become familiar with their new abode. She told them to sit at the table and she would serve them supper first, as there were neither room nor chairs enough for everyone.

While the children were having their supper, Anne explained to them that Tommy would sleep with Bill, in his small room at the rear of the house, and Jane would share a bed with Margaret at first, and with Anne when the baby arrived. When the children finished supper, they were helped to their rooms. Bill showed Tommy where to stow his things. He pointed out the water pitcher with a drinking glass, the wash basin, and the chamber pot. Anne did the same for Jane and Margaret.

After tucking the children safely into bed, Margaret kissed each one, and told them to sleep well. She then returned to the kitchen where the four family members sat at the small table to enjoy the first supper they had had together alone since they left Boston two years before. The conversation during supper covered many subjects, from the work at the mines, to Anne's washing and ironing business for Kelley's hotel and for the many single men in town, to Bill's work at the hotel stable. Anne told of the many proposals of marriage she had received from lonely men, young and old, none of which appealed to her.

Margaret mentioned her surprise at the large number of men she had noticed standing about as they came through Inskip. Anne explained that news of new gold and silver strikes in Nevada and Idaho territories had attracted many California gold seekers, but because of the deep snow blocking the trail in the high mountains, they had become stranded in Inskip. She cautioned Margaret not to become frightened during the night if she heard loud unfamiliar noises. The packers had long strings of pack mules and donkeys staked out in the nearby hills. Sometimes several of them would start braying and the entire herd would join in, creating ear splitting sounds, especially around sunrise.

True to Anne's word, the following morning was heralded by roosters crowing, accompanied by donkeys and mules braying and, to a lessor degree, dogs barking.

Tom and Bill, up at the crack of dawn, started a fire in the cook stove for Anne. She made coffee and, after they had downed a quick cup, they fetched buckets of water from the Dewey Ditch, which came from the Feather River and was used in the sluicing operations of nearby mines. While Anne made their breakfast of pancakes and eggs, they filled the tubs for her daily washing. By the time Margaret dressed, breakfast was ready. She set the table, and while they ate, the boys explained how the water in the ditch was diverted into long wooden sluice boxes. The miners dumped loads of gravel into them, and the water washed the dirt and gravel over riffles in the bottom of the box where the heavy gold would deposit behind the riffles. Once or twice a day, the mine boss collected the deposits in the riffles and panned the gold flakes and nuggets from the heavy black sand.

After her brothers left for their work, Margaret sat with Anne at the table and talked until the children awoke. Anne poured each child a glass of warm milk and gave them each a bowl of mush.

When they finished eating, Margaret gathered the dishes, while Anne carried the chamber pots to the outhouse where they were emptied and cleaned with water from a bucket. Leaving a small amount of water in the bottom of each chamber pot, she returned them to their places under the beds.

On an ordinary day, Anne usually started preparations for washing during breakfast, when she would put the wash-boiler on the stove along with two kettles of water that Tom and Bill had carried from Dewey's ditch. After the breakfast dishes were done, she would take an empty bucket in each hand, walk to the ditch, fill the buckets, and would return with the water to be heated for rinsing. When the boiling, scrubbing, and rinsing were finished, the wet clothes were wrung out by hand before being hung outside to dry on lines strung between pine trees. In stormy weather, lines were strung up in the kitchen where heat from the wood stove helped the drying.

Anne would then take care of the housekeeping chores and have a quick snack of lunch: usually a cup of milk and a slice or two of bread and butter, occasionally with a little honey on the bread. Her afternoon would be spent ironing. It was a constant chore carrying in wood to keep the fire going in the stove where the flat irons were heated.

That day, Anne had set aside a portion of the wash not urgently needed, in order to have time during the afternoon to accompany Margaret to meet Dr. Carter and his wife, Louise. Anne wanted the doctor to become familiar with Margaret's pregnancy, and to check her general physical condition.

On their afternoon walk to the doctor's house, they stopped at the Kelley Hotel to deliver a large bundle of finished laundry. Margaret was introduced to Mr. Kelley, the owner, and she mentioned that after her child was born she would be available for any respectable women's work that he might have. She told him of her experience in hotel and boarding house work.

Margaret found Dr. Carter and his wife to be a pleasant young couple. The doctor practiced out of his home, and appeared to be well informed regarding the problems that might be encountered during childbirth, and the precautions that should be observed prior to the birth. He admitted, however, that most of his practice involved treating accident victims from the mines, persons injured by horses or in horsedrawn vehicle accidents, and an occasional case of food poisoning or a gunshot wound. Because of the small number of women in Inskip, he had only a couple of childbirths since beginning his practice. He assured Margaret that she was in good health and, having had no problems with her other two children, she should have a normal birth within a few weeks.

Thus assured that Margaret's condition appeared normal, mother and daughter stopped at the store of R.C. Gridley to pick up some groceries. Margaret was introduced to Mrs. Gridley, who assisted her husband in the store: a likable young woman only six years older than herself. Conversing with Mrs. Gridley while Anne was picking out a few items needed. Margaret let it be known that after the baby was born she would be looking for some type of work, and she would be grateful if Mrs. Gridley would advise her of any jobs she heard of.

During the following three weeks, Margaret suffered the discomforts that accompany pregnancies in the last stages. She tried in all ways possible to assist her mother with her washing, but some days all she could manage was to stoke the fire under the wash boiler. Other times she would fold the linens and men's shirts that Anne had ironed, or set the table and clear it after meals.

During the second and third weeks of March, as the

sunshine and warm spring breezes prevailed, the packers, weary from their long delay by the winter storms became restless. They began to contemplate trying to break open the mountain trail. Two of the packers with experience on the Dogtown-Humbug trail agreed to make up a small train of their best behaved and most rugged animals, and try to break through the snow drifts blocking the trail near the summit. They agreed that, if they were successful in opening the trail to General Wood and W.B. Long's place in Humbug Valley, they would leave their mules there and return for their remaining animals and cargo. On returning, they would advise the other packers of the conditions they could expect to find on the trail.

It was well after dark five days later when the two weary packers rode their tired saddle horses back into Inskip, with the news they had succeeded in reaching W.B. Long's place with their nearly exhausted mules. They were two and a half days floundering through the snow drifts, and had been successful in breaking open the trail, allowing then to make it back to Inskip in one long hard day in the saddle.

The information they got at Long's was that he and General Wood had opened the trail from Humbug to Joshua C. Abbott's ranch in Big Meadows the week before, Josh Abbott had assured them the trail from the headwaters of Clear Creek to the junction of the Noble Emigrant Trail would present only a minimal number of snow drifts, if indeed someone had not already broken through them to Roop's Town(Susanville). From there on the high desert environment did not usually have a great amount of snow.

Activity in Inskip the next few days resembled a wild rodeo, as the packers rushed to assemble their mules and horses, fit and load the pack saddles, and settle up their bills with the Inskip merchants, hotels, saloons and stables. Inskip residents were awakened well before dawn the next four or five days by the braying mules and whinnying horses, protesting the pack saddles and halters forced upon them after several weeks of freedom from those burdens.

During all this wild confusion, Margaret awoke on April Fools Day of 1860 with severe cramps, which she recognized as the beginning of labor pains. Anne immediately started timing them and laying out clean linens. Bill helped Tommy and Jane to dress and fed them breakfast. He told them their mother was in pain and would spend the day in bed, and that they should not go into her bedroom until they were told it was all right to do so. He had the children move their playthings into his room.

About 7:00 A.M. Margaret's pains were coming frequently. Anne instructed Bill to stop by Dr. Carter's house on his way to work, and tell him Margaret's labor had started, and ask him to come and attend her. By the time Dr. Carter arrived at the house, Anne had everything under control. The doctor checked Margaret's pulse and temperature, and had hardly started to feel her abdomen for movement when things began to take their natural course. Anne soon had a grip on the small infant and was pulling gently, telling Margaret to push. Dr. Carter watched Anne's actions, and wiped the sweat from Margaret's brow with a cool, damp cloth. The doctor took the baby from Anne and, holding it by its feet, gently tapped it on the back to start it breathing. He laid it on a towel and sponged it off with a warm, damp cloth, informing Margaret she had a fine healthy boy.

Dr. Carter checked Margaret over and, satisfied that she had come through the ordeal with no ill effects, congratulated Anne on her fine performance as a midwife. He advised Margaret to rest, and said that he would stop by again before nightfall to check on her and the baby.

After the doctor left, Margaret dozed off, exhausted. Anne went to Bill's room where Jane and Tommy were playing, and told them their mother had given birth to a baby boy. She said that their mother was sleeping, but if they would be very quiet and not wake her or the baby, Anne would take them in to see their new brother. She took the two small children by the hand and led them to the bedroom door, admonishing them again to be very quiet and just look at the baby, not to touch it or ask questions while in the room. Both children stood wide-eyed beside the cradle for several minutes, viewing the small bundle of humanity sleeping peaceably. Anne then led them back out of the bedroom. In the kitchen she answered their questions the best she could, gave each some bread and milk, and then let them go outside to play in the fresh mountain sunshine.

The next few days, as Margaret was recuperating, nursing the baby, and assuring Jane and Tommy the baby would not replace them or her love for them, a number of the Inskip housewives stopped by to see the newborn. A baby was quite a novelty in the rustic mining town. Among the ladies that came was Dr. Carter's wife Louise, and Amanda Dickey, the merchant's wife, who brought a small blanket as a gift. Margaret Coleman from the hotel brought a rattle she had bought on a trip to Marysville. Even Emily Lathrope, the saloon keeper's wife, stopped in to see the infant. Of course their Boston friend Louise Kellog made several stops to visit with Anne and Margaret, and to see the new baby.

The most unusual and surprising visitor came about two weeks later. A woman Margaret had never seen or met drove up in front of the house in a camp wagon loaded with supplies and household goods. Tied behind was a fine Spanish saddle horse, and attached to the sides of the wagon were several cages, containing nearly a dozen live chickens. Margaret watched from the window as the woman, who was dressed in overalls and wore a red bandanna around her head, tied the reins around the wagon's brake handle and climbed down from the wagon seat with a halter rope in her hand. This she attached to the horses' bridles and tied to the hitching post in front of the house.

Margaret called her mother to the window to observe the rather tall, raw-boned, suntanned woman in her late twenties or early thirties who was headed for the front door. She had been momentarily distracted by Jane and Tommy who were playing outside, peeping curiously at her and the strange wagon with the attached chicken coops. They were not certain of the gender of the person, but responded to her friendly "Howdy" with a childish "Hello."

Anne informed Margaret that the visitor was Eliza Philbrook, who no doubt was on her way to the high mountain meadows where she and her husband, Alonzo Philbrook, grazed their cattle during the summer months. Anne had met Eliza one day last summer in Charles B. Clark's store, Eliza was a pleasant housewife who seemed to be lonesome, and welcomed the opportunity to talk with another woman. Her mannish ways had been acquired from working with men and livestock most of her life.

Before Anne could say anything more, Eliza was knocking on the door. Anne greeted Eliza with a friendly welcome. Once inside Anne introduced Eliza to her daughter, informing her that Margaret and the children were staying with her for awhile. Anne, whose tea kettle was always hot, invited Eliza and Margaret into the kitchen where she would brew some tea.

As soon as they were seated, Eliza began asking

questions about the children: what were their names? How old were they? Where were they from? Clearly this roughly dressed, coarse-appearing person had a great liking for children. Margaret, in turn, asked if Eliza had any children. Seeing the sorrowful expression that came over the latter's face, Margaret was sorry she had asked. Eliza explained that at first she and Alonzo were so busy struggling to build up a herd of livestock and develop the acreage they had claimed along Mud Creek, north of General Bidwell's Ranchero Chico, that they had put off having a family. Now that they were getting established with winter quarters in the valley and summer range in the high mountain meadows, they had not yet been blessed with a child.

Margaret then related her experience of having two children in what she thought was a permanent and secure marriage, only to have her husband and sole support of her children snatched from her by the angel of death. Then, after entering what again appeared to be a promising marriage, she discovered too late that the man who had promised to help provide for her and the children was unreliable.

Anne went into the bedroom and returned with the baby, who was fussing for some nourishment. She showed him to Eliza, who was very obviously smitten and who watched with great interest as Margaret nursed the child. Eliza asked many questions concerning the care of the baby. When he finished nursing, she asked if she could hold him for a few minutes. Margaret handed her the baby, and it was very clear to Anne and Margaret that this woman had a great natural desire to have a child of her own. They had no doubt but that she would make a good, loving mother. Eliza Philbrook continued to coddle the baby, gently rocking as it dozed.

Eliza told Anne and Margaret that her husband Alonzo, with a couple of Indian vaqueros, had started two days earlier to drive their herd of eighty cattle to the summer pasture. She had closed their cabin and corral gates at Mud Creek, finished loading the supplies and hand tools in the wagon, and started on the trail of the drive, getting ahead of the herd near Dogtown.

She told them that the past three years it had been their practice to set up a summer camp near a spring in the high meadows. This year, however, they had made an arrangement with Mr. John H. Smith, the owner of the Chaparral House, to headquarter there. Chaparral House had been built by Smith and Ball in 1857. It was a large, two-story, summertime inn, four miles northeast of Inskip on the Inskip-Humbug pack trail. Because the inn was conveniently located adjacent to the Philbrook's summer range lands, Alonzo and Eliza had agreed to operate it, paying John Smith a percentage of the receipts.

Eliza reluctantly handed the sleeping baby back to Margaret, who excused herself, took the baby into the bedroom, and placed it in the cradle.

Anne and Eliza continued to discuss Philbrook's new venture operating the inn. Eventually, their conversation turned back to Margaret and the children. Anne pointed out the problems Margaret was going to have earning a livelihood and taking care of three small children at the same time.

Eliza finally said she would have to be on her way, as she was to meet Mr. Smith at Chaparral House that afternoon to check over the condition of the facilities. Her husband Alonzo was due to arrive there the next day with their herd, and they wanted to be able to approve and sign the lease agreement.

Eliza indicated she would be coming back to Inskip in a few days for supplies, and would stop to see the baby. Margaret was in the bedroom with the baby, and was alerted by the sound of Jane and Tommy's voices in the yard yelling "good-bye." She watched from the window as Eliza untied the horses, climbed aboard the odd-looking wagon, and, with a snap and tug on the reins that demonstrated the expertise of an experienced teamster; turned the team from the hitching post and started up the winding trail toward Chaparral House.

The following mid-morning Alonzo Philbrook, accompanied by his dog and two Indian vaqueros, herded the eighty head of cattle through the town of Inskip, whistling and yelling at the herd to keep them moving along the town's dusty street. Two local dogs, aroused by the commotion, concluded it their duty to challenge Alonzo's dog. The ensuing fight attracted the attention of spectators from the local saloons. Alonzo turned his Spanish horse and rode back from the drove. A couple of well placed snaps with his bullwhip dispersed the two mongrel challengers. Not making a particularly good showing against the tough cow dog, they needed little encouragement to leave the scene.

Margaret stood at the window with Jane and Tommy, watching the bellowing drove going by the house. She noticed that they stopped up the trail at the Dewey Ditch to drink. The vaqueros, with their snapping whips and loud shouts worked to move the herd along.

Days passed slowly for Margaret as she regained her strength and began to move about the small community in search of work. She contacted all five hotel owners and informed them of her past experience in hotel and boarding house work. She also contacted the five merchants including Charles B. Clark, who was also her mother's landlord. Margaret explained to each that she needed employment to support herself and children, and would appreciate any work they might have.

All treated the young widow with great respect, but were unable to offer much encouragement. They advised her that some of the mines were becoming worked out and miners were leaving the area to try their luck in Nevada and Idaho. With the mountain trail now open, the stranded packers had left town. Only a few pack-trains a week passed through Inskip, and they didn't contribute much to the town's business. Discouraged in her search for employment, Margaret began to consider returning to San Francisco, where more opportunities for work existed.

Her brother Tom was also cognizant of the depleting placer deposits. He had begun to express his concern that he might have to leave the area when news broke in the small community that, Falkner and his son, while clearing a rock slide out of San Dewey's ditch, had discovered a quartz vein containing visible quantities of gold. Sam Dewey, who had been experiencing diminishing sales of water, was quick to encourage the unemployed miners and prospectors to search the area for other veins bearing gold.

# CHAPTER VI

## CHAPARRAL HOUSE

One morning during the first week of May 1960, the Philbrooks' odd-looking camp wagon tied up in front of Anne's house. This time the wagon was minus the chicken coops and the saddle horse, and the wagon box appeared to be empty. Eliza Philbrook made her way to the door where she was greeted by Margaret, who escorted her to the kitchen where Anne was busy with a stick, turning the clothes in the wash-boiler.

The original Chaparral House (built around 1857). Photo from file of *Paradise Fact and Folklore*, Vol. 20, No. 1, courtesy Paradise Historical Society.

Eliza's first inquiry was about the baby: she wanted to know how he was doing and if he had been named. Then she asked whether Margaret had found suitable employment. She was advised that the baby was doing fine. A name had not yet been decided upon, and Margaret had found nothing in the way of work.

Eliza told Margaret that with more prospectors in the area searching for veins of gold ore, and with stagecoach service once or twice a week expected to start soon, she and Alonzo could use some help in operating Chaparral House. They had concluded that if they had someone experienced with preparing and serving meals and overseeing household chores, Eliza would have time to take care of the small vegetable garden and the chickens, milk the cow, and do the washing. Alonzo could take care of the bar and, with the help of the vaqueros, water and feed the stage teams and pack animals expected to stop at Chaparral House.

Eliza told Margaret that they could not pay much cash, but would provide board and room for her and the children, if she would be interested in such an arrangement.

Margaret felt she was imposing on Anne and upsetting their living arrangement, but she asked Eliza for a little time to think it over. Eliza had come to Inskip for supplies, and told Margaret she would stop on her way out of town to see if she had any other questions.

After Eliza left, Margaret and Anne talked over the unexpected offer. Anne was reluctant to have Margaret and the children leave, but she admitted that the possibility of finding work in Inskip, where the children could be with Margaret, was slim. Neither Margaret nor Anne had ever seen Chaparral House. Anne had been told that John H. Smith and a Mr. Ball had claimed three hundred acres of land on the Humbug trail and, in 1857, had built a large, two story inn, speculating that the trail would become a stage road. Anne had heard that Mr. Ball sold his interest to a Mr. Wright, who operated it in 1858, and that Smith bought out Wright in 1859. John Smith had operated Chaparral House last year.

Alonzo Philbrook pastured his cattle on and around the acreage claimed by Smith during the summer months. So Smith's proposal to Philbrook that he headquarter at Chaparral House, and operate the inn during the summer season, appeared to be in the best interests of both parties. Anne indicated she was skeptical of the Philbrooks' ability to operate a public house because of their lack of experience.

Nevertheless, with no other immediate prospects for employment, Margaret concluded she might as well give Chaparral House a try. When Eliza stopped by on her way out of Inskip, Margaret quizzed her on the type of accommodations she and the children would have, and what she could expect in remuneration, if she accepted their offer.

She agreed to a trial period of thirty days, with the provision that if everything was mutually satisfactory at that time she would remain the full season, until the storms closed them down. Margaret told Eliza she would need at least a day to pack the children's things and her clothes. Eliza agreed that she or Alonzo would bring the wagon down the next day, and transport Margaret and the children to Chaparral House.

It was mid-day when the Philbrooks' wagon arrived at Anne's home. Alonzo Philbrook was the driver that day. He carried their luggage and loaded it in the wagon, then returned to the house for the baby's crib. Jane and Tommy were lifted into the wagon and instructed to sit on a piece of luggage behind the wagon seat. Alonzo then helped Margaret up onto the seat. Anne handed the baby, whom she had been holding, to Margaret. The two children waved to their grandmother as Alonzo started the team up the road for the four and a half mile ride over the winding mountain trail.

During the ride, Margaret became acquainted with Alonzo, a nearly six-foot-tall, thirty-year-old native of Louisiana who still had his Southern drawl. Margaret had seen him only through the dust when he drove his herd of cattle by the house in Inskip.

On their arrival at Chaparral House, Margaret was surprised by the size of the structure. The wide covered porches around three sides of the building made it appear larger than she had expected, and most impressive in that remote wilderness. Just beyond the main building, alongside the wagon road, was a watering trough fed by a freshwater spring. The spring was also the source of water for Chaparral House. Beyond the watering trough was a barn used to store a supply of hay and oats, and to stable the guests' horses in inclement weather. During good weather the horses and mules were usually staked out in the meadow across the road. Inside the house Margaret found a lobby where travelers could relax and rest during their stop to water and rest the horses. Meals were served in the adjacent dining room, which was furnished with two long tables and wooden benches. A small corner bar in the lobby was attended by Alonzo, when his services were not required outside overseeing the care of the travelers' livestock.

At the rear of the building, beyond the dining room, was the kitchen. Against one wall was a large cast-iron cook stove with a large bake oven. In the center of the room was a large work table used to prepare and dish up meals. The other side of the room served as a wash area for dishes, and doubled as a laundry room for the linens used in the guests' rooms as well as for personal items.

Eliza led Margaret and the children to a bedroom just off the kitchen, which had an outside door providing direct access to the path that led to the outhouse behind the main building. The outhouse had two doors one marked "MEN" and one marked "WOMEN"; with a partition down the middle.

The bedroom had a double bed for Margaret and Jane, and a cot along one wall for Thomas. There was plenty of room for the baby's crib in the large room. A burlap curtain hung from a wooden rod across one corner of the room, providing a makeshift clothes closet: a set of wooden shelves nearby, also with a burlap curtain, served as storage for small items, baby clothes, and toilet articles. It was a far cry from the furnishings among which Margaret was raised in Boston, but practical for the rugged surroundings in which she now found herself.

The next week, Margaret and Eliza spent most of the daylight hours readying Chaparral House for business. They began by washing the many windows in the building inside and out. Then they wiped down the walls and ceiling for cobwebs, aired out and repaired the straw mattresses, washed down the iron and wooden bedsteads, and applied a strong coating of turpentine to discourage an infiltration of bedbugs and lice. They finished the week by giving the wooden floors a thorough scrubbing.

Meanwhile Alonzo and the Indian vaqueros were busy repairing the corral fences and the barn doors, cleaning out the spring, and generally sprucing up the outside areas. Occasionally they would ride their mounts out through the mountain meadows to check on the cattle grazing on the sweet young meadow grasses. They would round up any that had strayed too far from the main herd, watching for any signs of predators, human or animal. Some of the native Indians still

roamed the area, and had been known to help themselves to a stray young calf. Once in awhile a hungry
mountain lion would kill and devour an unsuspecting
calf, leaving the carcass for the buzzards to strip. A
combination of factors—keeping the herd close together, the vaqueros' unannounced presence, and an
occasional well-placed rifle shot—had the effect of discouraging predators. It was also the duty of Alonzo or
one of the vaqueros, while on their roundup, to keep
Chaparral House supplied with fresh venison.

As the weather warmed, activities at Chaparral
House began to pick up. Saddle and pack-trains carrying miners and their supplies to Nevada or Idaho began
making overnight stops at Chaparral House. Due in
part to the new lode mining boom along the ridge, the
hotels in Dogtown and Inskip were filling to capacity
nightly, so the latecomers began to proceed on to Chaparral House.

Margaret's pleasant personality and cheerful greet-
ing to all the patrons quickly won confidence and respect. Alonzo and Eliza were overwhelmed by her com-
petence in the kitchen and dining room, a knowledge
and ability that far over-shadowed their meager experience in that business. The Philbrooks soon began to
withdraw to the more monotonous tasks, and allowed
Margaret to assume more of the personal contacts with
the quests. To free Margaret for her additional responsibilities, Eliza began to take over the baby's care: bath-
ing, dressing, changing, washing diapers and rocking
him to sleep. When the opportunity presented itself,
Alonzo enjoyed playing with the infant. He also helped
entertain Jane and Tommy, showing them around the
barn and corral, and pointing out to them the different
kinds of birds, squirrels, chipmunks, lizards, snakes
and other wildlife that ventured near Chaparral House.
He cautioned them to stay away from snakes, and to

call him or one of the vaqueros if they saw one with rattles on its tail.

One afternoon, a week or so later, two young cattle-men driving a heavy-duty-wagon loaded with hardware, building supplies, and camping provisions made a stop at Chaparral House. They entered the lobby after turn-ing the wagon and horses over to the vaqueros, and were greeted with a friendly welcome by Margaret.

The eldest of the two, probably in his middle thir-ties, had an accent which she judged to be Swedish or Norwegian. He signed the register as Peter Olsen from Oroville. The younger man signed in as Reuben Stover from Marysville. Both men were surprised to find such an attractive young woman in such a remote area. They were instantly attracted by her New England accent and her refined manners. She, in turn, found them quite attractive for westerners.

When she inquired their destination, they were more than willing to continue talking with the cheerful young woman. She learned that Peter Olsen was a cattle rancher near Oroville, and that Reuben Stover and his brothers raised cattle on their ranch near Marysville.

They were on their way to Big Meadows near the headwaters of the Feather River to set up a summer camp, where the year before they drove their cattle for grazing. They had located land in the northwest arm of Big Meadows, and planned to make it their permanent ranch.

Alonzo Philbrook, entering the lobby, was glad to see the two young men he had met the year before, and joined in the conversation. Alonzo mentioned that Big Meadows seemed a long way to drive cattle to summer pasture. They informed him of their intention to build ranch houses and to make Big Meadows their perma-nent home. However, for a year or two, until they could build adequate housing and install the necessary ranch facilities, they planned to spend the winter back in the valley. They said that after they had set up temporary camps on their claims, Reuben planned to stay and look after both camps, while Peter would return to the valley and help Reuben's brother, Thad Stover, drive their herds over the mountains to Big Meadows. Peter Olsen told Alonzo they had talked with Joshua C. Abbott, who had lived in Big Meadows for five years, and he told them his cattle had no problems surviving the winters when fed hay during the periods of heavy snows.

Margaret, who had only heard of Big Meadows as a point on the trail from Oroville to Roop's Town (Susanville), remarked that she had never seen Big Meadows and wondered what it was like. They explained that it was a large valley about twenty miles long and six miles wide, surrounded by mountains covered with pine and fir trees. The North Fork of the Feather River, abundant with native trout, flowed the entire length of the valley. Lush meadows provided food for the herds of mule tail and black tail deer, and was nesting ground for dove, quail, and waterfowl. Because of the high elevation, the winter storms, and the isolated location, settlers had been discouraged from building permanent homes.

At that time, Joshua C. Abbott was the only permanent settler. They expected others to soon follow, as all the mountain valleys were beginning to become inhabited. W.B. Long and Allen Wood had settled in Humbug Valley, and this year they were going to rebuild their hotel which burned in 1858. They expected to get the lumber from Jones and Wallach, who had built a small sawmill nearby.

Margaret was impressed by the description the two cattlemen had given of the Big Meadows. She returned to her duties, leaving Alonzo to converse with the young

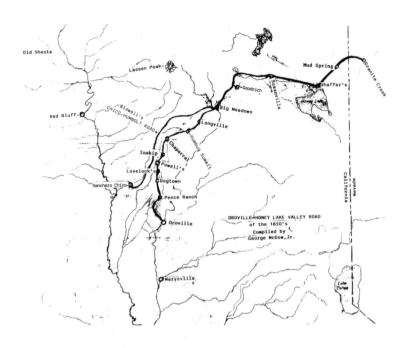

men. As she prepared the evening meal, her mind kept recalling the things the two young men had said about grazing cattle on the unlimited grasses. Alonzo and Eliza had spoken earlier about raising cattle in the Sacramento Valley, feeding them free of cost on the green winter grass. She could see a lot of potential in the cattle business. If a person could acquire the necessary livestock to start a herd, graze it on the vast public land, and thin the herd in the fall and spring by selling the prime beef cattle (always keeping the young heifers and calves in order to increase the herd by a few each year), in no time at all one could start one's own livestock ranch. This thought was to remain in her mind and develop over the years to come.

Olsen and Stover inquired about the road conditions ahead, and Alonzo told them the packers had not reported any trouble. He thought that, with caution, they could get through by removing some rocks and maybe filling a few holes.

After breakfast the next morning both Olsen and Stover complimented Margaret, whom they started calling "Maggie," on the good food and the comfortable bed they had enjoyed. Olsen was quick to remind her that he would be returning in a few days on his way to join the cattle drive, and he would stop again for another meal.

Margaret, sensing the admiration the Philbrooks had acquired for the baby, and still unsettled about a name for the infant, asked them if they had any objections to her naming the babe Alonzo, after Mr. Philbrook. They both expressed delight at the idea. Thus, Charles Kelly's son became known as Alonzo Rodgester Kelly.

Word of the excellent services, good food, and refreshments available at Chaparral House was passed quickly by the pack-train operators and travelers. Within weeks, Chaparral House's reputation was known from Oroville to Roop's Town in Honey Lake Valley. By early summer, the weekly stage and pack-train operators had adjusted their schedules for noontime or overnight stops at Chaparral House. At times when more than one saddle train stopped overnight the guests would overflow the sleeping quarters, requiring the latecomers to spread their blankets on the large porch or in the barn. Regardless of how many showed up for breakfast, Margaret, with Eliza's help, always had enough pancakes and hot biscuits to satisfy the hungry travelers, although there were times when a second table setting was necessary. Such were the conditions at Chaparral House on May 3, 1860, as Margaret quietly observed her twenty-second birthday. A note from her mother, carried by a pack-train operator, wishing her a happy birthday was the only unusual event of the day.

The following week, a few light rigs traveled the road. Most stopped for food and refreshment, some for overnight lodging. The packers and saddle-train riders stopped to stretch their legs, water the animals, and partake of some refreshments. Most of the time they camped along the trail when night fell.

Near the end of the week, Peter Olsen rode in on his saddle horse, staying overnight again. He was anxious to engage "Maggie," as he and others had begun to call her, in conversation. This time he informed her that neither he or Reuben Stover were married, and he hinted that they hoped to find good wives after they got established in Big Meadows.

Maggie sensed that Peter wanted to talk with her in a more personal manner, but she did not wish to mislead the handsome Norwegian into thinking that she might be interested in a romantic adventure. She was much relieved when Alonzo came into the lobby, giving her an excuse to retire to the kitchen where Eliza was beginning the preparation for the evening meal.

The next morning, Peter Olsen told Maggie he would try to stop in again when he and Thad Stover brought their herds by.

A few days later, W.B. Long came down the road from Humbug Valley driving a heavy wagon with two two-horse teams. One team was pulling the empty wagon and leading the second team, which could be hooked to the wagon when loaded, thus making a four-horse team. He stopped at Chaparral House for a noon meal and to visit with Alonzo, to learn what success he was having running an inn. Long was on his way to Oroville to purchase a load of hardware, windows, doors, and other fixtures he needed to rebuild the hotel destroyed by fire two years before. He advised Alonzo that, although the road was badly rutted in some places, it was passable for large wagons. He stated that he and Allen Wood planned to do some work on the road as soon as they could get the hotel building finished.

During the first week in June, Peter Olsen, Thad Stover, and three vaqueros drove the bellowing herd of Olsen and Stover's cattle up the road by Chaparral House. After their herds were well up the Humbug Road, Olsen and Thad Stover left the vaqueros to drive the herds, while they rode back to Chaparral House for a couple of shots of whiskey. Peter Olsen asked to see Maggie, on the pretext of wanting to introduce Thad Stover to her.

Alonzo called Maggie in from the dining room, where she had been wiping off the dust that had filtered in from the passing drove of cattle. Peter, feeling the effects of the Chaparral House whiskey, grabbed Maggie in a big hug like a long-lost sweetheart. Surprised at the unexpected action of the dusty; unshaven Norwegian, she pulled away. Alonzo, attempting to ease the situation, called Maggie over to the bar and introduced her to Thad Stover, who engaged her in conversation.

Peter realized he had acted a little boldly, but made no effort to apologize. When the two young men were ready to continue on their way, Maggie followed them out onto the porch and waved to them as they mounted their horses and galloped off in pursuit of their cattle.

Packers, returning from the mining camps in Nevada with their strings of horses and mules, began to arrive at Chaparral House on their way to Oroville and Marysville for supplies. They told of the Indian uprising in western Nevada. The Indians had killed Dexter E. Demming, a settler in Willow Creek Valley north of Roop's Town, on January 12, 1860. The settlers in Honey Lake Valley and prospectors scattered through the Black Rock Desert country were uneasy and were taking extra precautions.

One packer who arrived about the middle of June, reported that Indians had killed a Mr. Cady and Joseph Blodgett in the lower end of Long Valley, while the two men were attempting to move their livestock out of the valley. They also said that "Moguannoga," the Paiute Chief at Humboldt Meadows, and nine of his braves burned a trading post on the Carson River and killed four whites.

The next packer to return reported that Major Ormsby and his company of militia had been lured into an entrapment by the Indians on May 12, 1860, about two miles south of Pyramid Lake. Major Ormsby and forty-five of his men were killed.

During the months of July and August, the saddle-trains returning from Nevada areas carried quite a few prospectors returning because they felt it too dangerous to continue their search in that area. Some of the men were among those who had wintered at Inskip awaiting the trail's opening. A few settlers from the eastern part of Honey Lake Valley who thought it prudent to move further west also came over the road. Most of the westbound travelers who stopped at Chaparral House had gruesome tales of the Indian uprising.

The thought of hostile Indians on the warpath only a little over a hundred miles to the east was disturbing and almost unbelievable to Maggie, who had only been exposed to the peaceful California foothill Indians. She began to question her rationale for leaving the highly civilized confines of Boston, and exposing herself and children to the hazards of life in the western wilderness.

Much to Maggie's relief, packers returning over the Humbug Road during September carried the happy news that Colonel F.W. Lander, whose company of men was working on the overland trail in the Black Rock Desert, had joined forces with Captain William Weatherlow and his Honey Lake Rangers in a expedition against the Indians. Many Indians lives were lost, as well as that of Alexander Painter, who was riding with Lander and Weatherlow. Colonel Lander finally succeeded in meeting with the Paiute Chief Winnemucca to discuss their many grievances. The Chief finally agreed that his Indians would stop killing whites if the United States would pay for the land the settlers had taken, and leave the Indians to fish in Pyramid Lake and hunt in the area.

The news of Winnemucca's promise was comforting to Maggie, even though those who carried the news expressed great skepticism that the Indians would adhere to their agreement.

The cold September nights began to have a colorful effect on the trees and bushes around Chaparral House. The green of summer turned to yellow, red, and gold shades of fall. Travel eastward to higher elevations slowed down, and patrons stopping were settlers and prospectors from the high mountains, beginning their fall trek back to the lower climes of the Sacramento Valley and the coast towns of San Francisco and Monterey.

Cattlemen with herds at pasture in the high mountains began to round up their cattle to start the long drive to lower elevations. Several of the drovers stopped at Chaparral House to refresh themselves, sometimes staying overnight before starting their roundup.

Alonzo was not in a great hurry to leave, but he and Eliza made plans to move their cattle to Mud Creek. He and the vaqueros spent a great deal of time in the saddle, scouting the meadows and canyons for miles around in search of strays. He pastured the herd on the west slope of the mountains, so that the drive to the valley would be all downhill, and he wouldn't have the risk of a high summit crossing that might become impassable if heavy snows should fall. As long as the cattle could find feed in the high meadows, extending departure would allow the fresh grass in the valley to grow and provide better forage.

Maggie sent her mother a note with a cattleman that she and the children would be moving back to Inskip around the first of November. She asked Anne to be on the lookout for any work that might be available to her. She'd heard that business was improving in town since the new gold strike.

Near the end of October, the first major storm gusted in from the Pacific, dropping much needed moisture in the Sacramento Valley. The cold mountain air combined with the moisture covered Chaparral House and the surrounding area with a few inches of snow, a timely warning that winter was not far behind.

Two days after the stormed cleared, the Stover brothers and Peter Olsen stopped to rest the cattle, and stayed just long enough for a cup of coffee and a piece of Maggie's rhubarb pie before moving on. They left with a promise to stop and see them all in the spring.

When business began to slow, Maggie and Eliza closed the upstairs rooms and packed the linens in rat-proof boxes, and Alonzo prepared the out-buildings for winter. Eliza spent a great deal of time caring for and playing with baby Alonzo, who was eight months old and beginning to observe things around him. It was quite obvious that she was going to miss the children, especially the baby. Eliza made it clear to Maggie that she wanted her and the children to be with them again the next summer.

Travel over the road had finally ceased for the winter, and the Philbrooks decided it was time to close Chaparral House. Alonzo and the vaqueros started the cattle moving just as the next storm system was moving in. Eliza left with the wagon ahead of the herd.

Anne was not surprised when, on November first, Eliza tied her team up in front of the house and helped Maggie, baby Alonzo, and the children out of the wagon. Anne came out and took the baby while Eliza helped Maggie unload their luggage and carry it into the house.

Anne insisted that Eliza have a spot of tea with them before leaving. During that time Eliza related to Anne how happy she was that Maggie and the children had spent the summer with them, adding that she and Alonzo were going to be very lonely this winter. Eliza had written Maggie a letter of recommendation commending her for having done an excellent job, but she confided to Anne that she hoped Maggie would be available to join them again the next summer.

When Eliza was ready to leave, she gave both Jane and Tommy a kiss on the cheek. Then she lifted Alonzo from his crib and, holding him closely, placed a big kiss on his head. Maggie thought she saw a tear in Eliza's eye as she bid them farewell.

During the next two weeks, Maggie canvassed all the respectable business places in Inskip in search of work. The meager cash earnings she had received in addition to room and board for her family would barely cover the cost of cloth to make new clothing and buy shoes for herself and the children. She assisted her mother, as much as possible, with her washing and ironing, and assumed much of the housework.

# CHAPTER VII

## CHARLES BATES CLARK

One day, as Maggie was preparing to leave the house to again contact the local business establishments in search of work, Anne asked her to take the rent payement to Mr. Charles B. Clark at his store. Anne had occasionally invited him to join them for a Sunday home-cooked meal, which he seemed to enjoy. She told Maggie to invite him to take Sunday dinner with them again that week.

Maggie delivered the rent payment to him along

C.B. Clark Store at Inskip, Butte County, California, 1860. Photo from Clark family album.

with her mother's invitation. At the same time, she reminded him that she was still looking for employment. The enterprising thirty-year-old man readily accepted Anne's invitation. He also told Maggie he might be able to offer her some work in the not-too-distant future.

Anne had introduced Maggie to Charles Clark when she first arrived in Inskip, but with the baby on her mind, she hadn't paid much attention to him. She noticed for the first time that he was a tall, good-looking, refined gentleman with a full beard that made him appear older than his years.

Maggie was pleased to learn that there was a possibility of going to work for him, and, anxious to make a good impression, she added a few refinements to the Sunday dinner. She assisted Anne by preparing and cooking a big pot of Boston baked beans, and made her special rhubarb pie.

Charles was greeted at the door that beautiful fall Sunday by Tom West. Tom and Bill engaged him in conversation about general activities around Inskip, the new mines opening up, and the conditions at the mine where Tom worked. Eventually the conversation turned to national problems: the election of Abraham Lincoln as president, and the speculation that some of the Southern States might secede from the Union after the inauguration the next March.

The women finished setting the food on the table, and called to the men that everything was ready. At the table, Anne turned the conversation to Maggie and the children. She asked Maggie to tell about some of the experiences they had the past summer at Chaparral House. Charles asked her to elaborate on some of the stories she had been told about the Indian uprising in Honey Lake Valley and Nevada territory. He expressed concern that further Indian problems might slow travel over the Oroville-Humboldt trail, just as it was beginning to be a lucrative business for establishments along the way, especially the merchants at Inskip.

Maggie inquired of Charles how long he had been in California. He told them he had come to California with his brothers in the fall of 1849 by ship from New York, where they had been raised. They had gone first to the Yuba gold fields, and from there they made their way to the Feather River area in the 1850s. His brothers, not having had much luck mining, had gone into business in Oroville. He had continued mining around the Lynchburg area, without a great deal of success. When he heard of the gold strike on the ridge in 1856, he acquired from his brothers as large a supply of mining equipment and supplies as he could pack on his three donkeys, and came up the ridge to Doc Enskeep's mining camp.

The miners who rushed to the ridge ahead of him were desperately in need of mining equipment and supplies. They offered him such good prices for his merchandise that he sold it all in two days, at a good profit. He then returned to Oroville, purchased two pack mules, and loaded all five animals with all they could carry. On his return to Enskeep's he set up shop in a tent. Within a week he was out of stock, so he again returned to Oroville. That time he was more selective, bringing back items that were most in demand. He found a constant need among the miners for shovels, picks, gold pans, rubber footwear, tough clothing items, and staple food supplies, which he tried to supply with weekly pack-train trips to Oroville. After operating out of the tent all winter in 1857, he hired some lumberjacks to whip-saw enough boards to build the storehouse where he was operating his store.

Charles Clark didn't need to ask Maggie about herself. Anne West, on several occasions while at his store buying foodstuff or paying her rent, had told him about

Maggie, her children, and the problems she had with her recent ex-husband. Charles had shown a great deal of interest in everything Anne had to say about Maggie.

Not wanting to wear out his welcome or appear overly anxious to spent time with Maggie, he thanked them for inviting him to partake of the delicious dinner. He bid them all a good day and returned to his storehouse.

A few days later, Charles sent word by one of the young boys in town that he would like to have Maggie come by the storehouse and talk with him. Maggie lost no time making herself as presentable as possible and getting down the street to Clark's storehouse. When she entered the storehouse, Charles introduced her to Joe, a slightly stooped man with a full white beard, well past the prime of life but of rugged build and still able to handle heavy objects. Charles told her that Joe was his helper and did a fine job of packing, loading and unloading the pack animals. He had not yet found a job too heavy for Joe to handle. However, Joe had little education and was unable to read the price of merchandise, add up a bill of sale, weigh out merchandise, or make change.

Charles then explained to Maggie that he had offered his business for sale, but had not yet negotiated a deal. However, he thought that by early spring some of the parties who had expressed an interest would take over the store. In the meantime he had been talking with Mr. R.P. Powell, who had a ranch about seven miles down the ridge, about buying land on which to build a sawmill, and for the timber. They had come to terms on 320 acres, and he had arranged for the sawmill machinery to be built in Sacramento.

Charles told Maggie that he needed someone to take care of the store, as most of his time this winter would be spent in building the sawmill. He explained that he thought she had enough experience serving the public, and that with a few days training, she could handle the store—especially during the winter, as most of the trade would be foodstuff and clothing items to local patrons. Joe could handle any heavy barrels or sacks of grain or flour that needed to be loaded or unloaded. He would come back at least one day a week and help her with ordering or anything else that needed to be done.

Maggie was quite surprised with the job offer, especially when Charles added that he would pay her $2.25 a day and give her a discount on all merchandise she bought, including that which Anne would need. That was considerably better than the $1.00 a day with board and room that she had made all summer. She understood, however, that the job would terminate any time a buyer for the store was found.

Maggie readily accepted his offer. She was on the job bright and early the next morning. It was quite confusing for her the first few days. Like all early trading posts, no goods were marked. The proprietor knew what he had paid for each item; he then doubled or tripled the cost when offering it to the customer, and oftentimes dickered over the price if the customer was inclined to do so.

Maggie was almost overwhelmed with the numerous articles. She at once made a list of all the items in the store, then reviewed the list with Charles, getting him to price each item. She then placed the list on the shelf under the counter where she could easily refer to it. Charles was pleased with the business-like manner with which she approached the work.

Maggie had never experienced handling gold dust and nuggets, the prevailing monetary units in use in the mining camp. Charles patiently demonstrated and explained how to weigh out gold on the scales, and how to check the dust and nuggets for purity. He also taught her the combination to the safe that was located in the back of the storehouse, cautioning her to be sure to keep it locked at all times. Although he had never been robbed, there was always the possibility of a hold-up or a fire.

Charles explained to Joe that he was going to be gone from the store most of the time, and that Maggie would handle all the sales and money. Joe was to do any heavy work that might be needed. Joe had a few reservations about taking orders from a woman; but it was only a few days before Maggie, with her enticing smile and cheerful disposition, had him won over, making him feel as though she were working for him.

Tending a store was a new experience for Maggie, but with Joe's help she had few problems. Charles, involved with the sawmill, spent less and less time at the store. By the middle of January 1861, he was only going back to Inskip on Sundays. He and Maggie went over the weeks' business and made a list of the supplies that needed replenishing. She gave him the excess gold and coins to deposit with the Wells Fargo in Oroville when he went there to pick up supplies for the store and the sawmill. If the items she needed were important, he'd send them up from Powell's Ranch; otherwise he brought them on his next trip.

Construction work progressed well on the sawmill. The machinery arrived by six-and eight-horse freight wagons, almost on schedule. The carpenters and millwrights lost little time because of weather or missing materials.

By the end of February, when Charles made his weekend appearances in Inskip, he seemed more interested in Maggie as a person than in her activities in handling the store business. After checking over the weeks' business, he suggested that she accompany him to Kelley's Hotel for dinner. The first week Maggie declined the invitation, using the excuse that Anne and the children were expecting her home. After a second refusal, Charles became more insistent. Maggie finally consented to join him the following week.

The next Sunday, Maggie accompanied him as she had promised. She was not surprised to find him to be a most courteous and pleasant escort, who easily engaged in conversation regarding events of social and political interest, both local and national. He seemed to enjoy exchanging the day-to-day personal experiences he was encountering, as well as listening to hers. Maggie and Charles became so caught up in their camaraderie that the sun began to get low in the west before they realized that dinner had been over for some time.

Maggie insisted that she must be getting home, and thanked Charles for the enjoyable afternoon. Not quite ready to break off the day's pleasantry, Charles insisted on walking her to Anne's house. Maggie urged him to get started for Powell's Ranch before it got dark, but Charles cast that off with the assertion that his horse knew the way and the moon would be out early.

The next two weeks followed the same pattern, with Charles and Maggie enjoying each other's company over dinner at Kelley's Hotel, followed by a casual walk the short distance to Anne's house.

April 1,1861, was the first birthday of baby Alonzo. It was also the day the proprietorship of Clark's store passed into other hands, and the new owner and his wife concluded they could handle the business by themselves. Maggie was sorry to loose the good wages but realized her employment had only been temporary.

Within a few days, Maggie received a message from Eliza Philbrook, mentioning they would be opening Chaparral House between the fifteenth and thirtieth of April. It was their wish that Maggie and the children would be part of their family again this season. Eliza stated that they expected travel over the road to increase and they could probably pay her a little more than last year.

Other business changes took place in Inskip during the spring of 1861. Peter Coleman advertised in the Butte Record that he had taken over the proprietorship of the Downer Hotel, advising the public he had refitted it with comfortable furniture, and that the table would be furnished with every staple food and luxury procurable in the market.

April also saw Clark's sawmill commence cutting lumber. As is the case with all mechanized operations, the sawmill's first week was fraught with minor delays and shutdowns for adjustments to the machinery, taking up stretched belts, and familiarizing the crew with their duties. By the tenth of the month, the sawmill was in full stride. Logs were being cut in the woods and skidded to the sawmill. The mill crew was becoming accustomed to their jobs, while the yard crews were getting their sore muscles toned, piling the heavy sugar pine boards for drying.

Charles' brothers from Oroville made a trip to Powell's Ranch to inspect the mill and the lumber being cut. They entered into an agreement with Charles to take all the boards and timbers he wished to supply to the lumber yard they were setting up in Oroville in conjunction with their mercantile business.

On April 23, 1861, news of the attack on Fort Sumpter reached Inskip. Within hours the word had spread throughout the town and nearby mines. The citizens began to gather in groups about town, talking about the attack and speculating on its consequences. They all gradually congregated in front of W.B. Lathrope's saloon. Following a suggestion that they organize and make a public statement of their feelings, they elected Jeff Scott president, Dr. J.S. Carter secretary, and prepared and passed unanimously the following resolutions.

RESOLVED: That as citizens of California, we disdain all sympathy with the assailants of Fort Sumpter and the leaders of the disunion element, and that our sympathies are with the Union men and loyal border states.

RESOLVED: That as citizens we will support no man for any office at our next election, who does not pledge himself to the Union, in an unequivocal manner.

RESOLVED: That as men we will sustain the President to the best of our ability, in all his efforts to maintain the law and Constitution of the United States.

RESOLVED: That these resolutions be published in *the Butte Record*.

Following the adoption of the resolutions, a good rousing Union speech was given by Samuel L. Dewey. Jeff Scott added some patriotic remarks, after which a motion to adjourn the meeting was made and thirty-four guns were fired for the Union. Some of the guns fired had not been out of their holsters in months.

Charles Clark heard the news of the Fort Sumpter attack from a mule skinner who had come from Oroville for a load of lumber. He decided to drive his buggy to Inskip and see what the reaction was to the event. Charles arrived after the big public meeting had adjourned. He conversed with Samuel Dewey and Dr. Carter, who were preparing a copy of the resolutions for dispatch to the *Butte Record*. Pleased to learn of the strong Union sentiment displayed by the townspeople, he decided while in town it was a good opportunity to visit Maggie and inform her what he had learned, although he was positive she already knew about the gathering and its results.

Arriving at Anne's house, he found Maggie helping her mother with the ironing, a chore she readily laid aside to visit with him. She inquired as to how things were going at the sawmill, and what had brought him to Inskip.

Charles owned three houses in Inskip that he rented, including Anne's house. This gave him the excuse that he was checking on his houses, and also that he wanted to see how the new owners at the store were doing. He also wondered how Maggie was doing, and whether she had found any prospects of employment.

Maggie advised him that the Philbrooks had asked her to return with them to Chaparral House again this summer, and she had accepted their offer. It had worked out well last year for the children, getting Jane and Tommy out from under Anne's feet; and too, being able to keep the baby with her solved a lot of problems that she would encounter on most jobs.

Charles told her he would be staying in Inskip overnight at Peter Coleman's newly furnished hotel, and he invited Maggie to go with him the next morning to visit his sawmill. He explained they could drive down in the morning, look at the operation, have lunch at Powell's, and come back to Inskip during the afternoon.

Maggie had heard so much about the sawmill while working at Charles' store that her curiosity had been aroused. When offered the opportunity to see for herself how a mill reduced the big sugar pine logs into boards she readily agreed, although she admitted to herself that the opportunity to spend time with Charles was an added inducement. Now that the baby had been fully weaned, and Anne was agreeable to taking care of the children, there was no reason not to accept his invitation.

Bright and early the next morning Charles drove his buggy to Anne's house. Maggie was ready for the day's outing. Kissing each of the children, she admonished them to be good and obey Anne. Scampering from the house like a fifteen-year-old, she almost jumped onto the buggy seat beside Charles.

It took nearly two hours for the horse to negotiate the crooked, rough, dirt mountain road down the ridge to Powell's Ranch, where R.P. Powell had established a small hotel and store to serve travelers and Clark's sawmill workers. Mr. Powell was now calling his place Powelltown. Close by was Charles' sawmill. The smoke from the steam boiler in the otherwise serene clear mountain air gave away the mill's location.

At the sawmill, Maggie's first sight was the ox teams dragging the huge sugar pine logs from the woods to the millyard. Charles pointed out how the log was rolled up onto the mill deck by means of a cable powered by a steam winch. Then by means of another cable the log was rolled onto a moving platform called a carriage. Two men rode on the carriage to control the log, moving it an inch each time the carriage moved past the big circular saw that cut a piece off the log. The sawn piece was then pushed by a man over to another saw called an edger, where the rough bark covered edges were cut off. Those strips, Charles said, were called edgings. They were piled on a two-wheeled cart which, when loaded, was pushed out to the steam boiler. There the boiler fireman chopped the edgings in lengths to fit in the boiler fire box for fuel.

The boards that had gone through the edger were pushed over to another saw that cut off the ragged or bark-covered ends. These they called trims, and were likewise taken to the boiler for fuel. Two men then grabbed the ends of the finished boards and piled them on a four-wheel cart which, when loaded, was pulled by a mule out of the mill to the drying yard. There, two more men called pilers stacked the boards in piles, with strips between each layer that let the air circulate in the pile, drying the boards.

Maggie remarked on the sweet, fresh smell of the newly cut sugar pine boards that permeated the air of the drying yard.

Charles explained that the one-inch boards would have to dry for about a month. The thicker boards would take longer. They would also cut some large timbers which usually were sold without drying, to be used for mine timbers, bridge or barn timbers.

The steam whistle signaled lunch time. As the sawyers shut down the machines in the mill, the silence seemed eerie after the loud whining saws and the roar of the whirling and snapping belts that operated the powerful machinery.

Charles escorted Maggie back to the buggy, near the little shack that served as an office. They then drove over to Powell's Hotel where they were able to freshen up and enjoy a noon lunch prepared by Mrs. Powell.

Maggie was impressed by the magnitude of the sawmill operation. She hadn't known what to expect, and what she saw far surpassed anything she had imagined. Although while at the store she had learned to appreciate Charles' business acumen, she now had an increased appreciation of his ingenuity, ability, and foresight.

Following lunch, they drove back to the sawmill where Charles checked on the crew to determine if any operating problems were encountered in starting the afternoon shift. With the sawmill functioning as it should, Charles returned to the buggy and started a leisurely drive back to Inskip.

By the time they reached Anne's house, Charles had answered a myriad of questions Maggie had asked about the sawmill business, his plans for the future, and his personal life: his family, his journey from New York to California, and his experiences in the gold fields. In fact, there was very little about Charles Clark that Maggie didn't know when she climbed down from the buggy with his assistance. She felt a pang of disappointment when Charles reluctantly loosened his strong grip on her hand.

Thanking him for a very pleasant day, she invited him to come in for a cup of tea. He declined the invitation, stating he wanted to get back to the sawmill before dark to see that things were in proper order for the next day's operation.

On the last day of April 1861, Eliza Philbrook again tied her team to the hitching post at Anne's house. The wagon was loaded with supplies, a milk cow tied behind and the chicken cages on the sides. Jane and Tommy ran out to meet her as she started toward the house. She stopped to give each a hug and a kiss. Maggie was waiting at the door to welcome her. Eliza's first inquiry, on entering the house, was concerning baby Alonzo. Being assured he was growing: fast and in good health, she accepted Anne's invitation to partake of some tea and loafcake. Maggie brought Alonzo, who was now one, out of the bedroom for Eliza to see. She insisted on holding him while they visited. After the three women had exchanged pleasantries, Eliza got around to asking Maggie if she was going to join them again that year. She mentioned that if travel increase over the road this summer, and business picked up as they expected, they would pay her an additional bonus at the end of the season.

Maggie had hoped for higher wages, but not having any better prospects, she agreed to the terms. Eliza told her she would be back the next afternoon, as she was anxious to get the house ready for opening.

The following day, Eliza arrived at the Wests' house shortly after noon. Anne assisted Maggie in getting her luggage to the wagon. Eliza helped Jane, now six, and Tommy, five, into the wagon, while Maggie returned to the house and carried out Alonzo, handing him to Anne to hold while she climbed onto the wagon seat. Anne placed a kiss on Alonzo's forehead before lifting him up to Maggie. She then leaned over the side of the wagon and kissed Jane and Tommy, bidding them all so long. Eliza turned the team and with a snap of the reins started them up the road. All on board the wagon waved to Anne, who returned their wave as she watched them depart.

Getting Chaparral House in readiness for the summer travelers was not the big undertaking it had been the year before. They had left it clean and in good order in the fall. A few mice had infiltrated through unobserved cracks and built nests in dark corners of a couple of cupboards; Otherwise things were just as they had left them. A good dusting and mopping was all that was required to put the house back in shape. By the time Alonzo arrived and pastured the cattle in the meadow along the creek, Eliza and Maggie had everything ready for the travelers. Alonzo and the vaqueros cleaned the grounds, put the barn and corral in order, cleaned out the spring, and stacked wood for the cook stove. When those chores were finished, they checked the wagon road to the summit, removing windblown trees and boulders, and filled the potholes.

At the summit they met Allen Wood and William B. Long from Humbug Valley who had been working to open the road from Long's place to the summit. They assured Alonzo it was now passable to Humbug, and they intended to check it to Big Meadows the next day. They all agreed that a team and wagon could now make it from Inskip to Humbug.

Alonzo informed Woods and Long of the attack on Fort Sumpter and other news that he had picked up in the valley. Having been isolated from civilization all winter, they were anxious to hear news from the outside world.

A few days later, Peter Olsen herded his cattle through the area. He stopped at Chaparral House, ostensibly for refreshments and a good home-cooked meal, although obviously his real purpose was to again see and visit with Maggie. A day or two later, Reuben and Thad Stover ran their herd of cattle by, stopping for the same purpose.

By the middle of May, word had reached Oroville and Marysville that the wagon road was open through to Honey Lake Valley and on eastward. The packers, anxious to get to Idaho and Nevada, began to arrive at Chaparral House with their strings of horses, mules, and saddle passengers who needed overnight accommodations. The Chaparral House's reputation for good food and comfortable lodging had not been forgotten. Business was good from the day the first pack-train arrived.

June 3rd, 1861, was a special day for Maggie: her twenty-third birthday. Shortly before noon, who should arrive by horse-and-buggy at Chaparral House but her mother Anne, accompanied by Charles Clark. Charles had invited Anne to join him for a visit to Maggie and the children on her birthday. He brought a large bouquet of spring flowers from Oroville. He prevailed upon Alonzo and Eliza Philbrook to let Maggie, Jane and Tommy have lunch with Anne and him. Eliza was happy to assume the cooking and serving duties for the noontime meal, which was usually only served to those working at the inn as most travelers were on the road at that time of day.

After lunch, Jane and Tommy showed Anne the

swing on the porch that Alonzo had fixed for them by attaching ropes to the porch rafters. Charles and Maggie remained alone at the table in the empty dining room, talking about her job and his sawmill.

Charles told Maggie how much he admired her, handed her a small, gift-wrapped package and said, "Happy Birthday." The gift was an expensive brooch. The surprise was so great that she sat and stared at it, unable to speak, for several moments. When she finally spoke, she told him it was so beautiful that words failed her. Suddenly she realized he had developed a stronger feeling for her than she had been aware of.

When Anne came in, Maggie showed her the brooch. She thought it very beautiful, and was surprised as Charles had made no mention of a gift on the buggy ride from Inskip. He had only mentioned the flowers he was bringing. Anne had suspected Charles had more than a friendly interest in her daughter.

Maggie proudly displayed her new birthday present to Eliza and Alonzo Philbrook, who exchanged knowing glances between themselves, and expressed their opinions on its beauty and the thoughtfulness of Charles. Alonzo excused himself to greet the first saddle-train of the day. While he helped the train operator with the animals, Eliza began registering and assigning rooms to the travelers.

Anne and Charles made preparations to start their journey back to Inskip. Maggie thanked Charles again for the lovely gift, and he said he would visit her again in a few weeks.

As more mines in Idaho and Nevada opened up and started producing, saddle-trains were stopping every two or three days at Chaparral House with money-thirsty miners, prospectors, traders, gamblers and female camp followers. They were anxious to get to the mining camps to ply their various trades. All were

treated with the same courtesy, respect and good service by the Philbrooks and Maggie. Alonzo Philbrook
did, however, clearly indicate to the obvious whores
that his rooms were for sleeping only, and they could
not practice their trade under his roof. He later confided to Eliza and Maggie that he really didn't know
what he could have done about it if one had engaged in
her trade.

This season some freighters started using oxen in
spans of four, six or eight to pull wagons with heavy
loads of supplies and mining machinery over the almost
impassable wagon road. There was talk among the
freighters that with some improvements on the road
they would consider starting regular stagecoach service
from Oroville through to Idaho.

One of the freighters left a copy of the weekly *Butte
Record*: for Alonzo to read. The Oroville paper con-
tained the following letter.

Bull Creek,
Butte County, Calif.
June 11, 1861
Residing and being closed in by the snow in
the above place all winter, on coming to the
town, of Inskip on Sunday to purchase provisions, I was agreeably surprised to see the business houses as well as the street literally
crowded with miners. I having been under the
impression that from a mining and business
point of view "Inskip was gone in." I inquired
the cause of so large a population and learned to
my satisfaction that the reduced price of water
and lumber, as well as other liberal inducements
held out to miners by the present enterprising
and liberal ditch proprietor, Mr. Samuel Dewey,
has encouraged the miners to prospect the hills

and ravines more thoroughly and extensively and as consequence they have struck good diggins in a good many places.

On the afternoon of Sunday, the miners held a large Union meeting at Ned Donahue's store and judging by the enthusiasm as well as the strong Union sentiment that prevailed at that meeting, Inskip would be rather a dangerous place, I think for a secessionist to utter or advance treasonable ideas. I returned to my cabin satisfied that sufficient loyal Union sentiment exists to save the country from any threatened danger.

Alonzo Philbrook, a native of Louisiana, read the above letter with interest and passed the paper to Eliza and Maggie to read. He made no statement or indication as to his personal feelings. No one ever knew whether he entertained any sympathy for the Southern cause; if so he kept it to himself.

Chaparral House teemed with activity all summer. On days the saddletrains stopped overnight, the small staff found themselves overwhelmed at mealtime. Maggie's duties gave her little time to attend baby Alonzo, and Eliza gladly took over for her, as well as giving much needed attention to Jane and Tommy when they were not playing with the vaqueros' children. The Mechoopda Indians were friendly and had been with Alonzo for many years, and every year they set up their teepees among the trees behind the inn. Eliza had taught the squaws how to do the laundry and the heavy cleaning chores. Maggie, although apprehensive at first, soon became comfortable having them around.

Charles Clark made several visits to Chaparral House during the summer, usually on a Sunday when business was slack. Maggie had more time available then to visit with him. Several times they took leisurely afternoon walks through the forest, watching the birds, squirrels, and deer as they flew or scurried from their path. Charles usually brought news or messages from Anne and her boys. Maggie in turn sometimes sent messages back by him.

By fall Maggie knew without a doubt that Charles had developed a serious interest in her. With two disappointing marriage experiences behind her, she had not intended to become involved again. She knew she should have discouraged his attention, but there was something about his refined manner and his tall handsome physique that she found irresistible. Each time they met, instead of discouraging his attention, she secretly rejoiced at being in his presence.

As winter approached, and the cattlemen moved their herds out of the mountains, Maggie and the Philbrooks began the process of closing the inn for the season. Maggie knew that their business had been greater than the year before and she began to wonder whether the Philbrooks would keep their promise of a bonus at the end of the season. No mention had been made concerning the extra money for several months. The last day, Alonzo presented her with twelve twenty-dollar gold coins, in addition to her regular last month's pay: a bonus of approximately a dollar a day for the season's work.

# CHAPTER VIII

# THE TURPENTINE VENTURE

Two weeks after Maggie returned to Inskip, Charles advised her he had sold the sawmill and its inventory to his brothers, John and Albert, the Oroville merchants. He had turned a nice profit, and in the spring he planned to go into the turpentine business. She was reasonably sure he would be successful in any business venture he undertook.

Turpentine was a commodity greatly in demand by both the Union and the Confederate forces for its medicinal qualities and for use in the manufacture of gunpowder.

Early miners had learned to distill raw turpentine for their own needs from the sap of the Ponderosa pine trees. Ponderosa pines graced the ridge and slopes between the Feather River and Butte Creek, and Charles believed he could produce turpentine on a large scale from the timber if he could find the proper buyers for his product.

It saddened Maggie to learn that he was going to San Francisco and would be away for some time. She had secretly hoped they would spend time together during the holiday season.

Charles had planned to ride his horse to Oroville, take the stage to Sacramento, and then the river boat to San Francisco. An unusually heavy rainfall had settled over the area, making travel by horseback miserable and uncomfortable, so he decided to ride the stage from

Inskip to Oroville. His plans were thwarted again when on his arrival there, he learned that the rains had flooded the road to Sacramento and the stage could no longer proceed.

Charles noticed a small flat-bottom boat unloading cargo at Oroville. Two days later, he and three others— miners of questionable character who were returning from the gold fields—were able to get passage aboard the small craft to Sacramento. The rains continued and the river was high. The trip down river was fast and in order to keep dry, Charles and the three miners were obliged to squeeze into the captain's small wheelhouse.

The captain used steam only when necessary to navigate away from snags and sand bars. Therefore he did not put in at Marysville, as usual, to take on wood for the boiler.

By the time they left the Feather River and entered the water of the Sacramento, it was beginning to get dark. The river was high but more serene, and the captain navigated the boat into the east bank at the small river town of Vernon, where he tied up for the night. They all went ashore to the hotel operated by David Abdill and C.C. Roth, where they were able to get a warm meal and lodging for the night.

The following morning, after taking aboard a number of sacks of wheat for a Sacramento grist mill and a supply of wood for boiler fuel, the little flat-bottom boat cast off and continued down river to Sacramento.

A day or two later, after spending some time in the small state capitol, Charles boarded the regular Sacramento-San Francisco paddlewheel steamer for a more comfortable voyage to his destination.

The storm continued intermittently, and by the time Christmas arrived Inskip was snowed in. Mines in the area were isolated, and miners who had made their way to Inskip on homemade snowshoes or Norwegian runners (skis) took lodging in the hotels. Gambling houses and saloons stayed open twenty-four hours a day. Some gambling tables were not always honest, and some saloonkeepers served whiskey not fully seasoned.

Christmas gifts at Anne's house were meager that year. Maggie had received no word from Charles. On New Years Day 1862, the family celebrated Jane's seventh birthday with a small cake at the noon meal.

Storms continued off and on for the next three weeks, replacing the snow that had melted during the few hours of daytime sunshine or warming winds. Around the middle of January, when the storms began to subside, one hardy mountaineer who had mastered the Norwegian runners skied down the wagon road until he ran out of the snow. Stashing his runners beside a tree, he continued on foot to the Pence ranch where he learned the rivers had overflowed, flooding all the low areas in the valley. He purchased as many supplies as Pence could spare and as he could carry, and the next morning he started back up the ridge. Traveling uphill was slow going. It was all he could do to reach Dog Town by nightfall. He sought shelter in the hotel and passed the word on the conditions in the valley.

At daylight, he set out on the last half of his journey. With short stops at Victor Poumarat's and R.P. Powell's, where he was given warm refreshments and took the opportunity to dry his socks and mittens. He reached Inskip shortly after dark.

When the community learned of the flooded conditions in the valley and at Oroville, they decided their isolation in the snow was not as objectionable as those enduring the wild raging flood waters. Maggie expressed her concern to family members about having no knowledge of Charles' whereabouts: whether he had reached his destination, or whether he might have been injured or even met his death in the flood waters that were reported between the foothills and San Francisco Bay.

It was after the first of February when Charles Clark finally arrived back in Sacramento by river boat. The flood waters had begun to subside, and clean up and repair work on streets and buildings was underway in the town. Crews with wagons and scrapers worked to fill the breach in the dike before another storm struck.

Charles finally found passage aboard the *Defiance*, a low draft stern-wheeler, headed for Marysville with a cargo destined for Marysville warehouses. When the *Defiance* reached Marysville, the captain told Charles that George Perkins, the Clark Brothers, and other Oroville merchants had made arrangements with the Marysville warehouses to buy part of the cargo he had aboard, to replace the stock they had lost in the flood.

The captain informed Charles that the *Defiance* would be working its way up the Feather River to Oroville. He warned Charles that navigation would be slow as they would have to be on constant alert for new snags, and bars, and changes in the river's course by the flood. Charles knew that the stages would be unable to transit the flooded areas and washed-out gullies, so he readily accepted the chance to return to Oroville aboard the *Defiance*.

The *Defiance* unloaded part of its cargo at Marysville and then continued up the shallow waters of the Feather River to deliver the rest to the Oroville merchants. It was a slow trip. The captain took every precaution to protect his boat by steering clear of the snags and sand bars that appeared in the shallow water. Sharp-eyed crewmen stood on the bow watching for underwater objects. Even with that precaution the boat sometimes rode up on a few hidden bars. In most cases, the captain was able to cut off power quickly and by reversing the direction of the paddlewheel; the boat could then free itself and back off the bar. Occasionally the boat became so tightly lodged it was necessary to string a line to the river bank and anchor it to a tree or some other substantial object. The steam winch on the boat could then pull it free. It took two full days to reach Oroville. The *Defiance* was the last steamboat to ever reach Oroville.

Charles was amazed at the extensive damage done by the flood waters. Many buildings were still anchored with large ropes that had kept them from floating away. The Chinatown area along the river had completely washed away, its adobe houses melted down by the high water.

While in Oroville, Charles visited with his brothers, and learned they had changed the name of their saw-mill to Clarks' "Sugar Pine Mill." He made a deal with them to tap the Ponderosa pine trees on their timber-land to recover sap for the turpentine still he planned to build.

All bridges had washed away during the flood. In order for Charles to get across the Feather River and resume his journey to Inskip, he hired a local Indian fisherman to convey him in his canoe. Once on the west bank, he set out on foot across country for the Pence Ranch, some twelve miles. At the Pence Ranch he borrowed a saddle horse for the last part of his trip. After a stop at Powelltown for rest and refreshments, he continued his journey. He arrived at Inskip after dark on February 11, 1862.

The following afternoon, fully rested and refreshed from his long tiring journey, he called at Anne's house. The family was celebrating Tommy's sixth birthday. Maggie was so relieved and delighted to see him when she answered his knock at the door that her emotions took over, and she threw her arms about him and placed a loving kiss on his cheek. He was surprised and pleased by her actions, and returned the embrace. When Maggie regained her composure, Charles reluctantly released his embrace. Overwhelmed with relief, Maggie had to fight the tears of joy that clouded her eyes.

After Charles had partaken of a generous slice of Tommy's birthday cake, he sat for the next two hours relating his unusual travel experiences.

When questioned as to the outcome of his business activities in San Francisco, he explained that he had found the exporters anxious to receive all the critical war supplies needed by the Union forces. They had readily agreed to purchase all the rosin and turpentine he could supply. Charles told them he had purchased the necessary material to build a still, together with the pails and barrels needed for gathering the sap and shipping the rosin and turpentine. The equipment was to be shipped as soon as the road from Marysville was dry and in shape for freight wagons to navigate.

Charles planned to hire the experienced, idle timber fallers to strip the bark and make the boxes in the Ponderosa pines. He had to use all his persuasive powers to convince the unemployed loggers that he was serious. Many local people thought it was a hair-brained scheme. But as long as he was willing to pay wages, and spring logging hadn't started, they agreed to accept his money.

The boxes were chopped into the tree, two to three inches deep, and six to eight inches wide. Into these, the sap would collect.

By late spring, he hoped to employ anyone, including women and older children, to gather the sap in pails and pour it in barrels for transporting to the still, where it would be distilled into turpentine and rosin. It would then be shipped in clean barrels to San Francisco.

By the time the regular logging jobs opened in the spring, the loggers had boxed several thousand Ponderosa pines on several hundred acres along the ridge. The exceedingly wet winter had provided an unusual large quantity of ground water, and the root system of the pines was converting it into sap that was already beginning to flow into the boxes.

Despite the fact that Charles had been busy with his turpentine still, he found time to make frequent forays to Inskip to visit Maggie and the children. He made no attempt to disguise his attraction for her, hinting in many ways that he was ready to consider matrimony.

Maggie, although extremely fond of Charles, was apprehensive that a third commitment might end in disaster as had her two previous marriages.

Maggie's mother subtly encouraged the union by pointing out Charles' many good qualities, and his charming manners. Her brother Tom held a great admiration for Charles' business acumen. This encouragement was not lost on Maggie.

On April 1, 1862, baby Alonzo's second birthday, the family gathered for an informal dinner, to which Charles had been invited. After enjoying the repast, he again broached the subject of marriage to Maggie. He reminded her that he had three houses in Inskip, and he would fix up any one of them in any way she wished. She could then stay at home and look after her children. Getting his new business started would require him to be away a great deal during the summer months, but he would be able to come home on Sundays; and by late fall, he should be at home most of the time.

Maggie was beginning to view a future with Charles with fewer reservations; however she had obligated herself to work during the summer for the Philbrooks at Chaparral House. Eliza had advised her by mail that because of the heavy winter storms and the late opening of the Humbug Summit Road, they would not open until May first. Maggie told Charles that, since by fall he would have his new business established and she would be under no further obligation to the Philbrooks, she thought they should wait and consider his proposal at that time.

Charles, sensing that Maggie was about to capitulate, was not willing to let the opportunity escape. He proposed to Maggie that they get married at once, telling her that she could order the furniture for the house and then go to Chaparral House for the summer. He would go up there and be with her as often as possible. When fall came, their home would be furnished and ready for them to move into.

Maggie agreed to the marriage proposal, but pleaded for time to prepare and explain to the children what changes they could expect. She also indicated she would like time to make herself a new wedding dress, and to get word to the Philbrooks that she might not be able to assist in opening Chaparral House, should they decide to open before May first.

They finally agreed on April 23, 1862, as the date they would marry. Maggie wrote a note to the Philbrooks advising them of her plans, and invited them to attend the wedding. During the ensuing three weeks, Maggie made her wedding dress with Anne's help. The gown was not a white frilly one, such as she had in Boston, but something that could be worn on other dress occasions.

Maggie, a very practical person, decided on the house that would be most suitable for their use. She gave a great deal of thought to the furnishings. Some of the furniture could be made by local carpenters, and the rest they would order from Marysville or Sacramento.

Eliza Philbrook, on her way to Chaparral House, stopped at Anne's place. She was accompanied by one of the Mechoopda Indian squaws, who was going to help clean and prepare Chaparral House for its opening.

Eliza was happy about Maggie's engagement, and told her that she and Alonzo were planning to attend the wedding. She told Maggie that she had made a new dress for the occasion.

Eliza offered to look after the children while Maggie and Charles were on their honeymoon. Maggie declined the offer, telling her that, if they decided on a honeymoon, the children would stay with Anne. Eliza pointed out that baby Alonzo would probably require more attention than Jane and Tommy and might interfere with their preparations, and she'd be more than happy to take him on ahead to Chaparral House. Anne suggested that it might be a good idea. After all, Eliza knew how to take care of him, and little Alonzo was familiar with Eliza and the surroundings at Chaparral House. Maggie felt the boy, now two, would pose no problem for the wedding, but did agree that if she and Charles decided to go on a honeymoon, she would let Eliza take baby Alonzo home with her after the wedding.

Charles was in love. He felt as though he was riding on a magic carpet as he drove through town in a rented surrey pulled by two perfectly matched chestnut horses with white blazes. He tied the team to the hitching post in front of Anne's house, which was already restraining Alonzo's team. Inside the house he was greeted by his friend, justice of the peace D.C. Downer, and other family friends.

At high noon on April 23, 1862, Justice Downer performed the short marriage ceremony. Charles invited the party to join them at Pete Coleman's hotel where he had arranged a special dinner to be served the wedding party. Afterward, when all the toasts were said and the delicious dinner consumed, Charles drove Maggie and Anne back to the house. There they met Eliza and Alonzo, who had gone ahead and were waiting to take baby Alonzo to Chaparral House. Maggie finally acquiesced about the baby, but the two older children were to stay with Anne until the newlyweds returned from their honeymoon.

Charles had reserved the best room in the house at the St. Nicholas Hotel in Oroville. They arrived there by the light of the moon. His brothers and their wives were waiting to greet them, and after two hours of joviality, the relatives departed.

The happy couple stayed two nights, then went on to Marysville where they spent the next two days browsing the stores in search of furniture for their new home.

On the return trip, they again spent the night at the St. Nicholas, and Charles learned the California Legislature had passed an act to encourage the production of turpentine. The state was offering premiums of $250 to $500 for the first ten to one hundred gallons of turpentine produced.

The newlyweds arrived back in Inskip on the last day of the month. The children and Anne greeted them with great joy. Anne had the Children's clothing packed, ready for their summer sojourn at Chaparral House.

The following morning, Charles drove his new family the four miles up the ridge to Chaparral House. Maggie found baby Alonzo enjoying the attention showered upon him by Eliza, Alonzo and the Mechoopda squaws. Charles unloaded the luggage and reluctantly bid them all good-bye. After a loving embrace and kiss from his bride he climbed into the surrey and waved as he drove back down the road alone.

Travelers were few the first week: one or two stockmen driving their herds to the mountain meadows dropped in. Alonzo asked the drovers to keep their herds on the road over the summit in order to break down the snow drifts, thus allowing the sun and air to melt the packed snow as rapidly as possible.

Maggie told the Philbrooks that while she and Charles were in Oroville, they learned that the U. S. Government had awarded a mail contract to Dean and Harbison to carry mail from Oroville to Susanville once a week, starting July first. They also had heard that Edward and Frank Davis had subcontracted the mail haul and were planning to operate a four-horse stage wagon during the summer.

Charles was kept busy near Powelltown constructing his turpentine still and arranging for the gathering of the pitch from the pine trees. He hoped to be the first producer to claim the premium offered by the state. Charles was not too busy, however, to ride his Spanish horse to Chaparral House two weeks later on Saturday to be with Maggie on Sunday.

While there, he discussed with Alonzo Philbrook the rumor he had heard of the Mill Creek Indians' recent depredations to the herds along Butte Creek and the valley foothills. Charles was concerned there might be some danger to his pitch gatherers out in the timber, as some were women and children. Alonzo advised him that he had not lost any stock to the marauders, but he had heard some of the herds in the meadows along Butte Creek had been pilfered of a few head.

On May 24, 1862, about a week after Charles returned to Powelltown, a report was received that Thomas Allen, a teamster employed by J.L. Keefer, had been killed and scalped on the Cohasset Road while hauling a load of lumber from Morrill's sawmill. A friendly Indian companion riding with him escaped, made his way to Keefer's ranch, and reported the savage attack.

On hearing the news, Mrs. Hickok, who lived nearby, became frightened for her children, who had gone on horseback to pick wild berries and had not returned. She enlisted the aid of friends, who found the bodies of her 16 and 13-year-old daughters punctured with arrows. Their horse and dog, also killed by arrows, were nearby.

On June 3, Maggie's twenty-fourth birthday, Charles again rode to Chaparral House to spend the day with Maggie, as he knew of her concern about the Indian raids. He tried to ease her anxiety by telling her the settlers would organize and take action to stop the Mill Creek's treachery.

On June 18, 1862, two weeks after Charles returned to Powelltown, a meeting of miners, settlers, and stockmen was held at the Forks of Butte Creek to consider ways of ending the depredations by the Mill Creek Indians. Charles attended the meeting at which those present adopted a written set of resolutions that outlined the dangers to the whites, and resolved to form an armed group to attack the Indians and punish them for their savage actions. A group of twenty-four armed settlers under the command of Captain Harmon "Hi" Good, a famous Indian fighter, was assembled and started in search of the marauding Mill Creek's. "Hi" Good and his volunteers soon located the Indians' camp and attacked, killing several Indians. Several more escaped. While searching for the Indians, they found the badly mutilated body of the little Hickok boy.

All the residents along the ridge had become conscious of the danger from the unfriendly Mill Creek Indians, and they began taking extra precautions for their safety, as well as for their livestock.

Maggie, accustomed to the friendly Mechoopda Indians, had heretofore not felt any qualms when Jane and Tommy roamed the area with the Indian children. She became extremely frightened, and restricted their activity to areas close to Chaparral House. She cautioned them to run to the house if they saw any strange Indians anywhere. That caused a few minutes of apprehension on several occasions during the summer, when unfamiliar Indians passed by. Each time this happened, Maggie felt uneasy until she could determine that the natives were either on missions for their employers or just hunting deer for the tribe's consumption.

On the afternoon of July first, right on schedule, the Davis brothers' mail stage stopped at Chaparral House to rest the horses and refresh the four passengers making the first mail run from Oroville to Susanville. The only mail addressed to Chaparral House was a letter from Charles to Maggie. After a half-hour stop, the stage resumed its journey over the Humbug summit to its overnight stop at Long's in Humbug Valley.

Charles was at Chaparral House on the morning of July fourth when the Davis brothers' stage made its return trip from Susanville. The driver brought news that the Indians were again driving off horses and cattle belonging to the settlers in Honey Lake and Long Valley, and some whites had been killed while pursuing the Indians. Some Indians had also been killed and several wounded in the skirmishes that followed. The stage driver also reported that in April Indians had burned the Mud Spring Station, a trading post and stopping place on the Humboldt Road several miles east of Susanville.

Charles told Maggie it was obvious that the increasing number of settlers in the Sierra foothills, Honey Lake and Long Valley, along with hundreds of prospectors scouring the Humboldt region of Nevada, were crowding the Indians out of their natural hunting grounds, and the Indians were retaliating. His explanation did little to soothe Maggie's concern for the safety of her children.

News of the gold and silver excitement in Idaho and the gold strike in the Black Hills of South Dakota had reached all parts of the nation. The Oroville-Idaho road, somewhat improved by the efforts of the settlers, was being used extensively by fortune-seekers and freight wagons going to that region.

Immigrants coming to California over the Noble Trail were turning south at the intersection, taking the Humbug road into the Sacramento Valley. Most of those weary travelers stopped to refresh themselves at both Longville and Chaparral House, where they enjoyed the services of the bar and dining room. They were tired of trail food and relished the opportunity to sit at a clean table, where Maggie's fine food and delicious pastries were set before them.

Occasionally Alonzo Philbrook would trade oxen and mules with the immigrants. He'd take their exhausted and sometimes lame animals along with as many dollars as he could get for a pair of his well-fed and well-rested animals. The worn out livestock would soon be hale and hearty again when turned out on the lush meadow grasses. He would then trade them to other immigrants. Everyone benefited, and Alonzo made a few extra dollars.

Charles tried to spend every Sunday with his family, but all week he was kept busy distilling the pitch collected by his crew. The pitch was flowing from the trees almost as fast as the collectors could make their rounds among the thick timber.

His first shipment of turpentine and rosin to the San Francisco exporters brought him a sum equal to his entire investment in the operation. He also hoped to receive additional premiums from the state.

By mid-August Charles made his second shipment of turpentine to San Francisco. With the operation running smoothly, he had more time to supervise improvements on his house in Inskip. He also had time to engage in community affairs, often meeting with D.C. Downer, Sam L. Dewey, Pete Coleman and other local leaders to discuss improvements at Inskip.

With the Davis brothers' stage carrying the mail through Inskip on their weekly run, the people of Inskip began to urge the community leaders to establish a post office. Charles Clark and D.C. Downer signed and submitted an application to the U.S. Postal Department in Washington D.C. requesting a post office be established at Inskip.

At the urging of R.P. Powell, Victor Poumarat, Sam Dewey and several other residents of Kimshew Township, Charles decided to run for the office of Justice of the Peace during the coming September election. This required him to make a trip to Oroville to file his nomination papers. He stopped at all the settlements and ranches along the way, and asked the men for their votes on election day.

In September 1862, Charles Clark and D.C. Downer were elected to the office of Justice of the Peace for Kimshew Township. They assumed the office on September 27, 1862. Charles lost no time in getting to Chaparral House to advise Maggie of his election. That weekend he spent an extra day at Chaparral House, claiming the need to relax after the election. However, it was obvious to all that he desired more time with his new wife.

As the fall weather cooled, the pines began to enter their dormant period and the sap flowed at a slower rate. There was only enough sap being collected to operate the still about three days a week. Charles calculated he would be able to distill enough turpentine for one more sizable shipment before the pitch ceased its season's flow from the trees.

At Chaparral House on October 12, 1862, Charles celebrated his thirty-second birthday. Maggie prepared a special birthday dinner for him. Later, in the privacy of their room, Maggie gave Charles his biggest birthday surprise. She informed him she had been having spells of morning sickness and was positive that she was pregnant. Charles was delighted, proclaiming the news to be the best birthday present he had ever received. He was concerned that Maggie might overdo in her work at Chaparral House, and suggested that she quit at once. Maggie assured him that she would be careful, that the season was nearly over and the inn would be closing soon.

By the first of November, travel over the Humbug Road had slowed to almost nothing. The cattlemen and their herds had all left, but the weekly mail stage, with fewer passengers, continued to stop at Chaparral House. Alonzo, fearing his livestock might be caught by a winter storm, began rounding up his herd. A week later he started his drive to the winter range at Mud Creek, adjoining General Bidwell's Rancho-Chico.

Eliza and Maggie closed Chaparral House for the winter, and Eliza drove Maggie and the children to their new home at Inskip. Maggie informed Eliza that due to the expected birth of a child in the spring, she would be unable to help them the next year. Eliza volunteered to assist Maggie in any way she could. She offered to look after the children during the birth of the new baby, or for as long thereafter as Maggie wished.

Anne helped Maggie get settled in her new home. She did the laundry for the family, and helped Maggie hem the lace curtain material she had bought in Oroville while on her honeymoon. Together they arranged the kitchen utensils on convenient shelves under and over the work benches.

Charles and the other business people on the ridge were pleased when notice was received on November 12, 1862, that the U.S. Postal Department had granted their request for a Post Office at Inskip. Samuel L. Dewey was appointed to serve as postmaster.

The Oroville-Susanville mail stage continued to

carry the mail until the roads got so bad the wagon could not negotiate them. After that, George Baker and A.L. Harper carried the mail over the route on horseback. During the dead of winter when the snow got deep, they used snowshoes. George Baker took the mail to Longville in Humbug Valley, and A.L. Harper carried it from there to Susanville.

# CHAPTER IX

## MAGGIE'S INSKIP HOME

The house that Charles prepared for Maggie was one of the best in Inskip. It was situated near the east edge of town on the stage road, a few doors from Anne's house. The rough, unpainted board-and-bat construction with a shake roof and bare plank floors and interior walls was typical of the early mining camp houses.

Maggie softened the rustic dwelling with lace curtains, gingham pillow covers, and table cloths. She made it a pleasant abode. It was quite a contrast to the accommodations she had to endure in Columbia, but a far cry from Boston's brick facade or San Francisco's wooden structures with the bay windows.

She was extremely happy to have such a successful and dedicated husband who provided her every need, and cared for her children as though they were his own.

Jane's eighth birthday came with the New Year of 1863. Maggie made a gala event of the occasion, inviting her mother and brothers to New Year's Day dinner. It was a day destined for national significance: President Abraham Lincoln issued his Emancipation Proclamation that day. News of the Proclamation, however, did not reach Inskip until a month later, a few days before the family was to celebrate Tommy's birthday in February.

During March, General Allen Wood, owner of the hotel in Humbug Valley, stopped at the Clark's residence on his return from a county supervisors' meeting in Oroville. He had gone there to petition for finances to repair and improve the road from Inskip to Longville. With the county funds he had been awarded, he planned to immediately hire a crew to widen and straighten the road over Humbug summit, so it would accommodate the larger Concord stage coaches planned for service during the coming season.

General Wood was optimistic that the increased use of the Oroville-Susanville route by travelers and freighters enroute to Nevada and Idaho mining areas held a great potential for growth for all businesses along the route. He planned to improve his facilities at Longville to better accommodate the teamsters, packers, and travelers.

General Wood was not the only one enthused about the potential of increased travel over the route. Oroville merchants had for several years been cognizant of the business generated by the packers and travelers enroute to the new mine fields. Six years earlier, in May 1857, they had sponsored a stage trip over what was then only a pack trail. It took them five days to reach Roop's Town (Susanville). The purpose of the stage trip had been to influence the U.S. Army to construct an immigrant road to connect with the Honey Lake-Oroville route. It was probably the influence of those Oroville merchants who brought about the generosity of the county supervisors when General Wood petitioned for funds to improve the road.

Charles, upon hearing of the possible development of the Oroville-Idaho route, and the rumors that California capitalists were planning to open transportation lines to the Boise Basin in Idaho, began to contemplate the possibilities that might exist for him, along the route.

General Wood told Charles that his son-in-law, William B. Long, had purchased the William Weatherlow ranch north of Susanville in Honey Lake Valley, and had moved his livestock to that area. William Long had reported that Susanville and Honey Lake Valley residents had staged a rebellion against paying taxes to Plumas County. They claimed their property was in Nevada, and not part of Plumas County. When the Plumas sheriff brought a posse to collect, a group of protesters barricaded themselves in Isaac Roop's old log cabin and exchanged shots with the posse for a day. Injuries occurred on both sides, and they finally declared a truce and agreed to ask the governor of California and the governor of Nevada to settle the dispute and establish the boundary.

The turpentine business had been so profitable the past year that Charles was starting up again. The sap was beginning to rise, and he was again training a crew of sap gatherers.

Maggie had been so busy making baby clothes and caring for her family that their first anniversary came before she knew it. They had a small family gathering at her mother's house on March 23, 1863. The following evening, Maggie began to experience the familiar feelings accompanying the onset of childbirth. Charles took Jane and Tommy to Anne's house to stay with the boys. He asked Anne to come and help with little Alonzo, and to help Maggie. By morning, Maggie was timing her pains and Anne had things prepared for the delivery. Shortly after daybreak, Charles went to the doctor's house to advise him the birth was imminent, and asked him to come and assist Anne.

So it was on April 25, 1863, two days following their first wedding anniversary, that Maggie gave birth to her fourth child, and Charles Clark's first. At Maggie's insistence the newborn boy was named for his father, and called "Charlie."

When Eliza Philbrook stopped at the Clark residence to give Alonzo a present for his third birthday, she was surprised to find that Maggie had given birth to another son. She was extremely happy for Maggie's good fortune, and she again offered to take the other children to Chaparral House for the summer. Maggie thanked her for the offer, but thought it would be too great an imposition. Eliza explained it would be no trouble because she had the help of the Indian squaws, and urged her to think it over. She gave little Alonzo a big hug and kiss and wished Maggie a speedy recovery, then continued on her way to Chaparral House.

Maggie realized it was going to be very lonely for the Philbrooks this season, and the children would miss the freedom around the inn. She felt compassion for Eliza, knowing that little Alonzo meant a great deal to her.

Charles had been occupied with the start-up of his turpentine business for the new season, and with his duties as Justice of the Peace. it was the latter part of April when he learned the California legislature had passed a bill on April 14, 1863, granting John Bidwell, J.C. Manderville, R.M. Cochran, and John Guill a franchise to construct a toll road from Bidwell's Rancho-Chico to Honey Lake on the eastern boundary of the state.

Inskip and other ridge communities did not become concerned until they learned that the Tehama County residents had bonded themselves for $40,000 $28,000 of this was to be used to build a wagon road from Red Bluff to Big Meadows where it would connect with the Oroville-Idaho road, thereby diverting traffic and business to Red Bluff.

Eliza stopped to see Maggie and the children around the middle of May. She told Maggie how much they missed her, and how lonely it was without the children around. She again offered to take little Alonzo for the rest of the summer.

Maggie had to admit that with the new baby, Charlie, she had her hands full. Anne was busy with her washing and ironing, and although she had offered to help, Maggie pointed out that she had little time to spare. Charles was kept busy with his turpentine still and was not able to give her the help she had expected, so she reluctantly agreed to let baby Alonzo go with Eliza for the rest of the summer.

Anne scolded her upon hearing of the decision, and Charles was upset that she had decided without consulting him. He said he would have gladly hired someone to come in and help with the housework. Maggie reminded both of them that Eliza and Alonzo doted on baby Alonzo since the day he was born, and she knew he would get the best of care.

A compromise was reached during the discussion when Maggie said they would visit little Alonzo every Sunday. They could have picnics in the meadows and Jane and Tommy could go wading in Philbrook Creek with their Mechoopda friends. The resolution turned out to be very agreeable for it gave Maggie and Eliza time to catch up on the happenings at Chaparral House, while Charles and Alonzo discussed politics and speculated on the latest news circulating about the new roads contemplated or under construction.

When word reached Inskip in late July that General U.S. Grant had captured Vicksburg on July 4, 1863, Charles was pleased. However, he suspected that when the war ended, production of turpentine in the Southern states would resume and the turpentine business in the west would slow down within a year of the war's end. With that possibility in mind, he began to push production as much as possible.

Others who had taken notice of Charles' success had erected small stills, and in some cases were stealing the sap from the trees Charles had boxed. He began to patrol his many acres of trees in order to protect his supply of pitch. Charles realized he was spending more time away from his family than he had promised Maggie.

In late August, he came to the conclusion that his profitable business venture in turpentine had an uncertain future and he thought it best to sell out and invest in something more permanent. As soon as the flow of sap began to slow, he offered his still for sale, along with his agreements for tapping the trees along the ridge.

W.G. Jones, who lived near Dogtown, a few miles down the ridge from Powelltown, made Charles an offer. They worked out a mutually agreeable arrangement, and Charles sold the still and equipment to him.

With the turpentine business behind him, Charles began to cast about in search of another business. He learned that General Bidwell intended to develop a new road from Chico along the ridge between Big and Little Chico Creeks, through Butte Meadows joining the Oroville-Idaho road in Big meadows. Bidwell's plan was to bypass the established settlements of Longville, Inskip, Powelltown, and the Lovelock and Pence Ranches, thereby diverting passenger travel and the freight business to his town of Chico. Charles could see that travel was going to be split between three roads into the Sacramento Valley. He began to turn his attention further east to the area of Honey Lake Valley.

The position of justice of the peace for Kimshew Township occupied some of his time, and required that he be available at Inskip. That interfered with his exploratory trips during the fall season of 1863.

Maggie, under the assumption that Charles would be home most of the time since he no longer had the turpentine business, insisted that little Alonzo return home. Eliza was visibly upset at having to give up the child, and relinquished him with great reluctance.

Little Alonzo made it clear he wasn't too happy about leaving Eliza. He had become accustomed to being coddled and fussed over by the Philbrooks and the Mechoopda children. But he settled down after a few days, and once again became part of the Clark family when Jane and Tommy included him in their play.

When the Philbrooks closed Chaparral House, Eliza dropped in to visit Maggie and told her how much she envied Maggie's ability to have children. She tarried longer than usual, holding and coddling baby Charlie and little Alonzo. She finally left with tears in her eyes and again reminded Maggie she would be more than happy to take care of all the children or any one of them next season. Maggie felt sorry for Eliza, who wanted children so badly but couldn't seem to have any of her own.

In the fall of 1863, storms were very light and the Humbug summit closed only a few days in late November. General Wood reduced his Oroville stage run to once a week. The Oroville-Susanville mail stage continued its weekly operation with four horses all winter.

Charles took advantage of the good weather and rode the stage over the mountains to Susanville. There he discussed with the town's merchants their views on any business ventures that might develop, either in town or along the Idaho route. He found most people optimistic about the future of the area. Good farm land close to town was all claimed and houses in town were all taken. One or two businesses were for sale but those were fly-by-night establishments that had sprung up during the past summer. They didn't appear to have any great potential.

After looking around Susanville and Honey Lake Valley for about a week, Charles left his name and mailing address with the town's founder, Isaac Roop, and with Isaac Jones, a young attorney. He told them that if any likely-looking business should be for sale or any nearby farm property should become available for rent or sale, he would like to know about it. He told them he had been favorably impressed with the town and would like to move his family to the area. Charles advised them he planned to return in the spring for another survey of the opportunities. At daylight the next morning he boarded the Oroville stage. He arrived back in Inskip the following day, after the regular overnight stop at General Wood's Longville Hotel.

At Inskip, Charles found things had been relatively quiet while he had been gone. Justice of the peace Downer had handled the few cases brought before the justice court during his absence. Charles told Maggie about Susanville and the conditions he had observed while there. He was greatly impressed with Honey Lake Valley as a place to live and raise a family. Although he had not located a business venture that appeared attractive, he felt that with the amount of travel and freight moving through the valley to Nevada and Idaho, some opportunity would eventually present itself. This seemed especially likely to happen after the new roads being built by Bidwell and Tehama County were completed.

Maggie was contented and completely happy taking care of her four children in Inskip. For the first time in her life she had a home of her own, furnished the way she wanted. She had her mother and brothers near by, and she had numerous friends. To start over in another frontier town even further removed from San Francisco and Sacramento, the only places the Boston-raised young woman considered the west coast's centers of civilization, did not set well.

When she became convinced that Charles had definitely made up his mind that his financial future lay elsewhere, she urged him to look westward before deciding their future. She pointed out to him that the California-Northern Railroad was scheduled to be completed to Oroville from Marysville the next year. No doubt new opportunities would develop around that area following the railroad's completion. Charles listened to Maggie's counsel, and agreed to spend some time in Oroville conferring with his brothers and other businessmen, in search of a financially rewarding venture.

His mind thoroughly made up that he would be leaving Inskip sooner or later, Charles submitted his resignation as justice of the peace for Kimshew Township, to the Butte County Board of Supervisors on December 17, 1863. W.P. Kelley of Inskip was appointed to fill out his unexpired term. Freed of all legal duties, Charles began to reconnoiter the Oroville and Marysville areas, searching for a challenging business venture that he might be able to build into a profitable business, as he had done with the Inskip store, the Powellton sawmill, and the turpentine distillery.

The holiday season was a happy time for the Clark family. With no business responsibilities except for his three houses, Charles was able to fully enjoy himself with Maggie and the children during the celebration of Christmas. He brought in a fir tree that they decorated with strings of popcorn and homemade cut-outs of angels and stars made by Maggie and Jane.

When the holiday season was over, the little tree with its homemade decorations, having contributed its share of holiday cheer, also contributed to the family's comfort by becoming fuel for the wood stove.

The winter, although cold, was exceedingly dry as there had been very little snowfall in the mountains. The stages continued to operate on a reduced schedule. Pack trains continued their operations, but the saddle trains did not. Few passengers were willing to endure the cold windy ride astride a horse or mule, when for a few extra dollars they could ride inside a stage coach.

During January and February 1864, Charles made it a point to talk with the stage drivers coming from Susanville, during their change of teams in Inskip, and with any of the passengers who had spent time in Honey Lake Valley. He questioned them about conditions there, and of their thoughts regarding the future of that area.

Charles also spent several days in Oroville searching for a likely looking business venture. He was among the crowd of well wishers and curious townspeople that assembled along the tracks of the California Northern Railroad on February 9, 1864, when the first train pulled into Oroville.

While in Oroville, Charles purchased a jack-knife and some fish-hooks as a birthday present for Tommy. Charles gave them to him on February 12, his eighth birthday, and told him when spring came he would take him fishing in one of the nearby creeks.

Near the end of February, Charles received a letter from Isaac Jones, the young Susanville attorney, informing him that he had learned Mr. E.H. Hosselkuss wanted to sell his livery stable in Susanville. One of his clients, Mr. William Wentworth was interested in purchasing the business, but not having sufficient funds, he was looking for a partner. Isaac Jones suggested that Charles come and meet Mr. Wentworth, and look over the business. He also stated there was a small farm available for rent on the edge of town, big enough to support a family with vegetables from the garden, and with pasture enough to maintain a milk cow. With poultry for eggs, he thought a family could live comfortably.

Charles again took the stage to Susanville, and with Isaac Jones' guidance, he looked over the farm. He met with William Wentworth, and agreed to join him as a partner in the livery stable business. With the deal for the livery stable and the farm secured, he rode the stage back to Inskip.

Charles enthusiastically related his dealings to Maggie. The farm was situated just outside the town of Susanville by a river which would provide adequate water for both livestock and a garden. The farm house was large and comfortable, and the best part of all was the school. The children would have other children to play with. The town, although small and rustic, was growing. He was informed that a Mr. J.I. Steward had acquired a large lot on Main Street and planned to erect a large hotel to accommodate the increasing number of persons traveling the road.

Maggie listened closely as Charles described Honey Lake Valley, with its vast area of lush meadow grasses that provided pasture and hay for hundreds of livestock raised by the settlers. He told her about the high, snow-capped, timbered mountains to the south, and the lower brush-covered mountains to the north and east providing thousands of acres of livestock range. He also mentioned the small settlements of Janesville and Richmond, and the growing town of Susanville at the western edge of the valley. There he told Maggie the river the length of the valley to Honey Lake exits from the vast timber-covered hills to the west.

Charles had also learned that General Bidwell and his associates, who had incorporated the Chico-Humboldt Wagon Road Company had a crew of Bidwell's Indians hard at work clearing the brush and shoveling out a trail that could be traversed by pack and saddle-trains, and that the trail would eventually be widened to accommodate wagons. The merchants in Susanville were quite excited that Bidwell's road would before long bring more travel over the route.

Charles told Maggie that he was convinced the farm

would provide them with ample produce to live on, and he was sure the livery stable was a good business venture.

It was the opportunity to enter the children in a regular school that convinced Maggie to pull up stakes at Inskip and move to the eastern side of the Sierras. Charles sent word to attorney Jones to notify Hosselkuss and Wentworth that he would be in Susanville in the next week or so to complete the transaction. Charles also passed the word around Inskip that all of his houses were for sale.

It was mid-March of 1864 when Charles Clark again arrived in Susanville. He found the residents full of anticipation that the legislature, in session at Sacramento, was going to form a new county to take Susanville out from under the jurisdiction of Plumas County, and give the area its own county government. The Susanville merchants were also anticipating that the county seat would be in their town and would bring them additional business.

During the time Charles was in Honey Lake Valley completing the arrangements to move his family to their new home, Eliza Philbrook, on her way to open Chaparral House, stopped by the Clarks' home in Inskip to visit Maggie and the children. She was surprised and greatly disappointed to learn that they would be moving out of the area. She told Maggie that she had planned to ask her to let little Alonzo spend the summer with them again this year. Instead she offered to look after all the children while the Clarks moved.

Maggie thanked her for the offer. She told her she would not know what the conditions might be until Charles returned, but she doubted they would need help with the children.

Maggie was anxiously waiting for the stage. When the driver pulled the four horses to a stop in front of the house, Charles stepped down and Maggie walked out to meet him. After embracing, they walked back to the house. He assured her that everything had worked out to their satisfaction. The farm house would be vacant and ready for occupancy the first week of April, which would give them ample time to get a garden planted. He had looked up their friend from Humbug Valley, William B. Long, at his new ranch north of Susanville, and Mr. Long had agreed to sell them a good milk cow.

Anne was greatly disappointed when she was informed that her daughter and family would be moving. Susanville was well over a hundred miles east, over a rugged, winding mountain road, and she was sure she would never see any of them again.

Little Alonzo Kelly had his fourth birthday on April 1, 1864, and Maggie was confronted with the problems of moving. The trip with a year-old baby, a four-year-old, and one eight and one nine-year-old was going to take at least three days of travel, providing the wagons didn't break down or the horses go lame. It was going to require camping out two nights somewhere along the road, and Maggie would have to cook their meals over a campfire, something she had not done since moving out of the tent in Columbia.

Maggie was busy separating the clothing and cookware they would need for the trip from the things that would go along with their furniture on General Wood's freight wagon when Eliza stopped by with a small birthday gift for little Alonzo. Maggie told Eliza about their plans and the hardships she foresaw. Eliza immediately offered to lighten her burden by taking little Alonzo off her hands. She said that after they were settled, Charles would probably be making trips back to Inskip on business and he could pick up Alonzo at that time.

Maggie called Charles into the house to listen to Eliza's proposition. He admitted the trip would be a little easier if they didn't have an active four-year-old to entertain. It would be hard on the child to sit still for the long period they'd be in the wagon.

Sensing they were about to weaken, Eliza strengthened her argument by promising to bring little Alonzo to see Anne whenever she came to town. Charles said they would like to give the proposal more thought and would let her know of their decision by stopping on the way over the mountains to either leave Alonzo with them, or explain why they decided to take him along in the wagon.

Anne, who was already upset about their moving, was further disturbed when she learned they were contemplating leaving the child with the Philbrooks when she was available. Maggie had to point out to her again that she had her hands full washing and ironing for her many customers, plus preparing meals for Tom, and Bill. Eliza would have the help of the Mechoopda squaws, and little Alonzo would have the Indian children to play with.

Maggie agonized over her dilemma while doing the final packing. She tried to visualize how they would be riding. She would have baby Charlie in her arms, Charles would drive the team, Jane and Tommy would sit on the seat behind, and Alonzo would have to fit between them,. Surely he would have to lie down and rest part of the time, and would no doubt be climbing over everything, subjecting himself to a possible fall from the wagon. Realizing that no four-year-old would sit for hours on a hard seat bouncing over a rough road, Maggie conceded it would be best to let Alonzo stay with the Philbrooks until she or Charles could come back and take him to Susanville by stage coach.

# CHAPTER X

## HONEY LAKE VALLEY—1864

At the first light of day, Charles helped General Allen Wood load the freight wagon. Maggie prepared an early breakfast, then packed the tin plates and utensils in a sack to be readily available for use along the road. Charles told Tommy to keep his fishhooks handy and they would try to catch some fish along the way.

By mid-morning everything was finally loaded and tied down for the long trip to Honey Lake Valley. General Wood headed out ahead. The heavily loaded freight wagon with its six-horse team would travel slower than the spring wagon with a four-horse team that would be carrying the family.

Anne came to see them off. She hugged and kissed each one, including her son-in-law. Then she stood beside the road waving as the wagon carrying Maggie and Charles and her four grandchildren moved up the road and disappeared around the first curve on its long journey over the mountains.

It was near noon when Charles pulled the team to a stop at Chaparral House. Eliza Philbrook ran down the steps to greet them. Alonzo, who had been working near the watering trough, held the team while the family alighted from the wagon. Maggie handed baby Charlie to Eliza to hold while she climbed down from the wagon. Eliza kissed and coddled the baby, insisting that her husband take a good look at the infant. Maggie told her that if she was still willing they would let little

Alonzo spend the next few weeks with them. When they got settled, one of them would come for him.

Eliza's face lit up and Alonzo Philbrook grinned broadly when he heard Maggie's words. Eliza insisted they all come in and have some of the apple strudel she had prepared.

Maggie and Charles lingered while Charles told the Philbrooks about the farm where they would be living and about the town of Susanville. Finally Charles said they had a lot of ground to cover before night and they had better leave.

Maggie called Jane and Tommy, who had gone up the hill to visit with the Indian children. She gave little Alonzo a hug and a big kiss, admonishing him to be a good boy. Eliza assured her again that the boy would get the best of care. Maggie knew the Philbrooks loved him as if he were their own, and she had nothing to worry about. Nevertheless, her eyes filled with tears. She said that one of them would return for him in the next few weeks.

Alonzo Philbrook handed the halter rope to Charles, and with a snap of the reins, the horses started up the road. It was a long, arduous ride over the twisting road along the creek tributary to the west branch of the Feather River, and two hours after leaving Chaparral House, they crossed the summit and began the long winding descent into the Humbug Valley basin. An hour later they reached Rock Creek, where they caught up with the freight wagon. General Wood stopped to let Charles pull his team alongside his to drink. Wood told them there were plenty of empty rooms at his Longville Hotel as the travel season had not yet begun, and rather than going to the trouble of making and breaking camp, they were welcome to stay the night as his guests. Charles consented with the understanding that he be allowed to pay for their meals. Wood agreed, and said his wife Mary would enjoy visiting with Maggie and the children. Then he started his six horses up the far bank of the creek.

When Charles' team finished drinking, he pulled the wagon ahead to the flat beyond the creek and stopped. Alighting from the wagon, he tied the lead horses to a nearby tree, then took the baby from Maggie and helped her down. Jane and Tommy had already climbed down and scampered back to the creek for a drink. Maggie got a cup out of the utensil sack and, with Charles carrying the baby, they walked back to the creek where they each enjoyed a cup of the clear, cool spring water. She gave the baby a few sips of the refreshing liquid, and after they stretched their legs a few minutes, Maggie called the children. They had to be on their way.

A half hour later they began to catch up with the freight wagon. It was well into the late afternoon when the two wagons arrived at Wood's hotel and stopped in front. Mary Wood was waiting on the porch to greet them. The General told her the Clarks were to be their guests that night, and he asked her to show Maggie and the children to their rooms. Maggie brought in their nightclothes and the toiletries they would need. While they were getting settled, the men drove the wagons to the side of the inn, unhitched the teams and turned them into the corral for the night.

The next morning as the first glimmer of daylight began to break through the trees on the eastern horizon, Maggie was awakened by the smell of coffee brewing. Charles was already outside harnessing the team. Maggie quickly dressed and aroused the children. While they dressed, she tended to baby Charlie. Then she went downstairs to assist Mary with the breakfast.

At breakfast, General Wood informed Maggie that she was no longer in Butte County. When they crossed

Humbug Summit the day before, they had entered Plumas County, and from now on she would be a resident of Plumas County. General Wood had not yet learned that the California Legislature had passed a bill on April 1, 1864, forming a new county on the eastern slope of the Sierra Nevada mountains, and it had been named Lassen County. They would learn this fact when they reached Susanville.

When breakfast was over, Charles helped the family into the wagon just as the road became clearly discernible in the early morning light. General Wood, who was familiar with the road, had departed in the freight wagon a half hour earlier.

Three hours later, after winding through pine-covered hills, they broke out into the vast, grass-covered expanse of Big Meadows. The horses stopped at the first small creek to drink, then started to feed on the sweet, young grass along the road. Both drivers had to use their whips to get them moving again.

Maggie gazed with amazement at the magnitude of the meadows and the beauty of the early spring wildflowers that carpeted the valley floor. They all shouted with glee each time they spotted a doe with her fawns crossing the meadow. Maggie remembered that Peter Olsen and Reuben Stover had described Big Meadows to her, but she had no idea that it was so large. She told Charles that they had said the meadows would support a thousand head of cattle and she now believed it. Charles pointed out a small plume of smoke arising eight or ten miles off to the northwest. The stage driver had told him that was the area in which Olsen and Stover had settled. Farther off in the distance, beyond the plume of smoke, rose a magnificent snow-covered mountain peak dwarfing all those surrounding it. Maggie was overcome by its majesty. Charles told her it was the landmark that Peter Lassen had used to guide his immigrant train over the mountains to California in 1848. It was called Lassen's Butte. Looking over his right shoulder, Charles pointed out a log cabin barely visible about three miles to the southeast, nestled against the timber bordering the meadow. It was the home of Josiah Abbott, the first settler in Big Meadows.

The wagons continued along the west side of the clear creek that flowed out of the mountains from the northeast. About noon they reached a ford across the creek where the road turned eastward into the pine covered hills.

Charles stopped, unhitched the horses and tethered them where they could graze on the lush grass. He told Tommy to see if he could catch a few grasshoppers and they would go fishing. Tommy took his hat and scouted the area while Charles cut two willows on which he attached a string with Tommy's fishhooks. Tommy returned with several grasshoppers in his hat.

A short distance down the creek below a riffle, Charles showed Tommy how to bait the hook and cast so the bait drifted into the pool. On Tommy's first cast, a nice brown trout grabbed the grasshopper. With a loud whoop, the boy jerked it out on the bank. Charles cut a forked willow stick and showed him how to remove the fish from the hook and string it on the stick.

Jane heard Tommy's joyous whoop and ran down to the creek, wanting to fish. She learned quickly, and Charles left the children to fish while he went to help Maggie prepare their lunch. Baby Charlie had dropped off to sleep so Maggie laid him on a blanket under the wagon seat in the shade. Charles built a fire and Maggie unpacked the frying pan and unwrapped some homemade bread she had brought along. By the time General Wood caught up with their camp, the children had a nice string of fish on the forked willow. It wasn't long before they were enjoying a delicious lunch, and they all agreed the fish were the tastiest that had ever been caught.

There was still a long way to go. They broke camp and the men rehitched the teams. General Wood left first. The road northeast became rougher and steeper as they entered the timber country and it did not become flat again until they reached Mountain Meadows. Nestled against the hills, a mile to the east, they caught a glimpse of C.P. and William Goodrich's cabin, the closest they had come to any human habitation since leaving General Wood's hotel.

The road became rough again as it wound its way around ridges of ancient lava flows from long-extinct volcanic eruptions. It was a tiresome ride filled with fine red dust kicked up by the horses' hoofs, causing the wheel horses to toss their heads and snort to clear their nostrils. Maggie had her hands full protecting the baby, and the others tied kerchiefs over the lower parts of their faces. Crossing small streams along the way became hazardous. The horses were so anxious to drink that the wheel horses tried to get ahead of the leaders, causing the wagon to rock perilously. Charles had to keep a tight rein on the team.

By late afternoon when the shadows began to lengthen, they finally broke out of the dusty road into the small meadow along the river that ran easterly toward Honey Lake Valley.

A short distance from the river, where the Oroville road connected with the Noble immigrant trail, Charles picked out a campsite that had obviously been used many times by immigrants before them. The horses were unharnessed and tethered in the grass near the river. Charles stretched a tarp, between trees to provide shelter over the family's bedrolls.

General Wood heated a bucket of water on the campfire, explaining that he thought they would all like some warm water to wash off the red dust they had endured that afternoon. He told Maggie that the worst was behind them, the road was nearly all downhill from there. The Noble Trail was well used, and with luck they should make Susanville by mid-day tomorrow.

While the children gathered firewood, Maggie prepared the evening meal, a stew made with beef jerky and root vegetables that had been stored in their cellar all winter.

When the children were out of earshot Maggie asked General Wood if there might be Indians around. He assured her that the local Indians in that area were friendly and they only came out at night to hunt when the moon was very bright. There would be a quarter noon that night and she had nothing to worry about.

It was getting dark by the time Maggie declared the stew ready. Charles put some large wood on the campfire, increasing the size of the flame to provide more light for the group as they sat around the fire pit and enjoyed their stew and bread. Maggie drained some of the broth from the stew and let it cool before feeding it to baby Charlie. The flames radiated heat that felt good as the evening mountain air began to cool.

Before turning in for the night, Maggie used the last of the hot water to wash the dishes. General Wood spread his bedroll beneath the freight wagon. The older children, tired from the long day, wrapped themselves in their blankets and were soon asleep.

When Maggie's chores were done, she and Charles settled down with baby Charlie between them. Somewhere in the trees an owl hooted, answered by the whinny of a horse. A lullaby made by the sound of water bubbling over rocks in the river soon had the exhausted group sleeping peacefully.

The sun was just peeking through the branches of the tall timber when chirping birds and excited squirrels scolded the intruders. Baby Charlie let it be known that he was hungry. While Maggie attended to his needs, Charles woke the children and gave them the chore of folding the blankets. General Wood had already started the fire and had water heating for coffee. Charles sliced bacon, and when Maggie finished feeding the baby, she made pancakes.

When breakfast was over, Maggie cleaned and packed the cookware and dishes. Charles and General Wood harnessed and hitched up the horses. They also checked the wagon brakes, as several accidents had been reported when going down the steep hill into Susanville. The momentum caused the heavy wagons to outrun the horses and overturn.

Before leaving, they made sure the campfire was out by dousing the fire pit with buckets of water. They were now on the last lap of their journey. Charles followed General Wood down the Noble Trail through the pine-covered plateau country that extended for many miles west of the valley. Deer scampered across the trail, often stopping some distance away in the forest to watch the curious contraption pulled by four large animals. The does tried to hide their fawns in the forest foliage.

The Clarks had been on the road about two hours when they came to a large spring gushing fresh clear water from the side of the hill and running across the road. General Wood had stopped to let his horses drink and to fill his water bag with the crystal clear water. He was ready to start on, and pulled his team ahead so that Charles' team could get to the water flowing across the road. He waved to them as he drove off.

Stopping the wagon just short of the flowing water where the horses could drink, Charles tied the reins to the brake handle. He helped his family alight from the wagon to quench their thirst with the beautiful clear water. After all had been thoroughly refreshed they continued on their way. About an hour later the road began to descend gradually. Charles checked his brake on each hill to be sure it would hold the wagon back on the long descent into Susanville.

Maggie had been anxious to get a view of the valley where she was to make her home. The close proximity of the trees blocked out any long range view, but between small openings in the timber she could get an occasional glimpse of the snow-covered peaks to the southeast. A short distance further along the road, a gully descending to the northeast provided her a glimpse of the mountains to the north. Charles began to exert more pressure on the brake to, hold the wagon back from the wheel horses as much as possible.

It was nearly noon when they suddenly broke out of the trees. Before them lay the vast expanse of Honey Lake Valley. A green mat of spring grasses sprinkled with interesting colorful designs created by wild spring flowers dramatically outlined by the high mountain range with its snow-capped peaks along the southern edge.

With the first view of the valley, Maggie realized they were entering the little town of Susanville. The town consisted of four blocks along the main street and was composed of ramshackled log and rough board buildings. Hand-painted signs indicated which were the stores and which were stables, or saloons, and there were one or two advertising rooms to rent. A flagpole without a flag stood in the middle of the street around which many horses and oxen belonging to an immigrant train rested as they waited for the wagonmaster to reassemble the train.

The framework for a large two-story building stood on the north side if the street. A crew of several men were at work fitting the framing timbers together. Charles told Maggie that was J.I. Steward's new hotel.

Kitty-corner from the hotel under construction was the livery stable in which Charles was now a partner. He pulled his team to a halt as his new partner, William Wentworth, came out to greet them. After introducing Maggie and the children he drove on to their new home.

Maggie and the children began to look through the house while Charles pulled their wagon around near the back door and unhitched the horses leading them to the corral. General Wood pulled the freight wagon up in front of the house where it would be convenient to unload. He and Charles started unloading the furniture and carrying it into the house. Maggie directed where each piece was to go. She requested they bring the kitchen table first, so she would have someplace to pile the utensils. Next she wanted the beds so that little Charlie would have a place to take a nap, and free her to

Susanville as the town appeared when Maggie arrived in 1864. Photo courtesy Lassen Historical Society, Susanville, California.

get things straightened out. Although tired from her long journey Maggie was glad to be in her new home.

# CHAPTER XI

## SUSANVILLE 1864

The first weeks in their new home on the outskirts of the small town were busy ones for the Clarks. Charles immediately purchased a milk cow and a few laying hens from William B. Long, and borrowed a plow from his neighbor with which to start his garden. When not at the livery stable, he spent his spare time planting vegetables and pruning the fruit trees on the property. Maggie was equally busy getting the house in order. The lace curtains she brought from Inskip had to be altered to fit the new windows, and she re-arranged the furniture many times. Their second anniversary and baby Charles' first birthday was taken note of only at the evening meal.

The election to be held on May 2, 1864, was the main topic of conversation among the residents of Susanville. It was the first election held in the newly formed county of Lassen, at which county officers were elected, and Susanville was chosen as the county seat.

By Maggie's twenty-sixth birthday on June 3, 1864, they were finally settled in their new home. Charles by that time had caught up with most of the major gardening chores, and was busily occupied assisting his partner with blacksmithing and horseshoeing at the livery stable.

Immigrant trains passing through town from the east brought some business to the livery stable when they paused to rest, replenish their supplies, and repair their wagons. Charles observed that the number of pack and saddle trains and wagons traveling from the Sacramento Valley to Nevada and Idaho mining districts was increasing. He surmised that as stage coach travel increased the hotel business would probably benefit the most from those passengers. He discussed his observations with Maggie as he kept his ear to the ground, in search of a more suitable venture in which to invest his capital.

By early summer Maggie determined that she was again heavy with child. This made taking care of baby Charlie difficult, and complicated her plans to travel back to Inskip to get little Alonzo Kelly. She sent Eliza Philbrook a note explaining that she was again pregnant and not able to travel, but she would arrange to have Charles or someone else come for him.

Charles entered into the civic activities of the area, that gave him the opportunity to become acquainted with most of the Honey Lake Valley residents. During the summer, he joined with about eighty other volunteers to form Cavalry Company A Fifth Brigade of the National Guard of California. The group took the name of "The Honey Lake Rangers." Because he was already in the livery stable business, Charles was elected farrier for the Company, an important position for a cavalry company as he was responsible for keeping the horses in healthy condition and properly shod.

In the fall of 1864, Maggie entered nine-year-old Jane and eight-year-old Tommy in their first year of public school, held in the town's new one-room schoolhouse.

Maggie received a letter from Eliza Philbrook informing her that little Alonzo was fine, that they had enjoyed having him with them all summer, and for Maggie not to worry if she or Charles were unable to get to Chaparral House before they closed. They would take Alonzo back to the valley with them, and would take good care of him all winter. Eliza also wrote they really had enjoyed watching him grow, and that they loved him as if he were their own son.

Maggie was relieved to learn that the Philbrooks would continue to take care of Alonzo during the coming winter, but she was very disturbed that Alonzo was slipping away from her. She realized he had become fond of the Philbrooks because of their pampering. Maggie sent Eliza some money by the stage driver to buy Alonzo new clothes when they got back to the valley.

During the month of October, J.B. Francis and E.D. Pierce from Idaho stopped over in Susanville while scouting out a route to the Sacramento Valley for a stage line. Charles learned of their interest in starting a through stage line, and began to give consideration to opportunities that might open along the route from Susanville to Idaho.

The prospects of through stage service to Idaho caused others to become interested in businesses that might benefit from the increased travel. When Mr. S.R. Wilson offered Charles $1,000, double what he had paid for his half interest in the livery stable eight months before, he agreed to sell. On November 4, 1864, he executed a deed to Mr. Wilson for his interest in the business.

Maggie's association with the Philbrooks and her conversations with Peter Olsen and the Stover brothers about the cattle business had impressed her. After viewing the large expanse of grasslands in Honey Lake Valley, she concluded cattle raising might be something to consider. She suggested that to Charles, and he discussed the livestock business with his cattleman friend, William B. Long, and with newly elected Lassen County Sheriff James D. Byers, who had been raising livestock for several years. Both advised Charles that nearly all the good grasslands had been claimed by early settlers, and the open range was already becoming overrun by the cattle and sheepmen. Some were driving their livestock to the area from winter ranges in the Sacramento Valley. Charles passed this information along to Maggie, and told her he felt he should stay with something he was better informed about.

Unlike the winter before, the storms of 1864-1865 came early and lingered later, depositing seven to ten feet of snow on the Humbug summit and shutting down all travel over the mountains.

Two years earlier, Congressman John Bidwell had been granted a franchise to build a road from Chico to the Humboldt mining district in Nevada. When Bidwell learned of Pierce and Francis's efforts to open a stage road to Idaho, he was so anxious to get the Idaho Stage Company to operate their saddle trains and stage coaches over his route that on January 25, 1865, he started out in a buggy, accompanied by E.D. Pierce, to transit the Chico-Humboldt route. They did not get far as the snow made the route impassable. Congressman Bidwell then hired two men to cross the mountains with Mr. Pierce on snow shoes.

When the three men arrived in Susanville, a number of local residents, including Charles Clark, joined the party and accompanied them over the route as far as Pueblo Valley near the Idaho border. Charles used the trip to determine where the stagecoaches would be stopping to change horses and refresh the passengers. He believed a new opportunity might develop along the proposed route.

The group stopped at Mud Spring Station on the way back. Charles met the owner, Patrick Bagin, who was in the process of rebuilding the station following the Indian raid that had burned it to the ground in

1859. Charles was impressed with the location, just west of the Nevada-California boundary, on both the Chico-Humboldt and Idaho stage routes. Bagin mentioned to Charles that he was thinking of selling the station.

When Charles returned home, he told Maggie of his observations and his conversation with Patrick Bagin. He told her that he believed the station had the potential to become a major stopping place once the stage company began its operation. Maggie expressed her concern that the location was in danger of further Indian attacks, and she questioned the advisability of investing in areas frequented by belligerent bands of renegade Indians.

On February 25, 1865, E.D. Pierce and John Bidwell's party left Susanville and started back to Chico. Pierce informed the Susanville residents that he had decided to start a saddle train from Chico to Idaho, running once a week until the snow melted in the mountains. Then they would operate a string of stage coaches.

Area residents later learned that Pierce chose the Chico route over the Red Bluff or Oroville route because John Bidwell offered to use his influence as congressman to get the U.S. Postal Department to award them a mail contract from Chico to Ruby City, Idaho. Bidwell was so determined to get the stage company to use his road that he also agreed to furnish livestock, hay, harness and stagecoaches for the company.

When Charles Clark learned that Pierce planned to start their saddle train the first part of March he contacted Patrick Bagin, and the two of them put together a deal for Charles to take over Mud Spring Station.

Maggie could not help with preparations to operate the station as she was expecting the birth of their second child. The care of little Charlie, not yet two years old, along with her homemaking chores was taking up all of her time.

Maggie had reason to feel relieved that Charles no longer held an interest in the livery stable. When on March 17, 1865, a fire started in the stable and spread to other buildings, consuming all but one of the old log and wooden buildings in the block. The following day she went into labor and gave birth to a daughter they named Harriet Eliza Clark.

Charles then hired an Indian woman to help Maggie with the housework, and her man to do the outdoor chores.

Lonesome to see her mother and her brothers in Inskip, Maggie longed to go after little Alonzo. It had been over a year since she left him with the Philbrooks. Charles was busy with his new business venture, and she was unable to leave her young children for the six-day stagecoach trip to Chaparral House and back. She had to be content with letters. She sent Eliza money to purchase necessities for Alonzo, who was now five.

On April 3, 1865, a month later than originally planned, the Idaho Stage Company's first saddle train to transit the Chico-Idaho road, under the command of Captain E.D. Pierce, left Bidwell's Rancho Chico. It arrived in Susanville four days later, with forty passengers riding the mules. On entering the town they were welcomed with a salute of blacksmith's anvils, and cheers from the local residents. It took the riders twenty-seven days to reach Ruby City, Idaho.

Charles Clark hired a horse wrangler and his wife to live at Mud Spring Station. The wrangler helped the packers with their strings of mules and horses, and his wife prepared food and served the travelers.

Word was received in Honey Lake Valley around the middle of April that General Lee had surrendered the Confederate forces at Appomattox on April 9, 1865, ending the War between the States. Patriotic feeling ran high throughout the valley. In a festive spirit, Charles and Maggie celebrated their wedding anniversary on April 23 with a dinner at the new Steward House dining room. Their spirits were dampened the following day, however, when word reached Susanville that President Lincoln had been assassinated on April 14, 1865.

Charles left town the next day with a load of supplies for Mud Spring Station, which was beginning to service several pack trains a week heading for the Humboldt mines or Idaho and Montana mining districts.

Immigrants traveling west over the Noble Trail

Historical marker on Noble Immigrant Trail and Humboldt-Idaho Road. Located along Highway 395 a few miles west of the old Mud Spring Stage Station. Photo by McDow 1992.

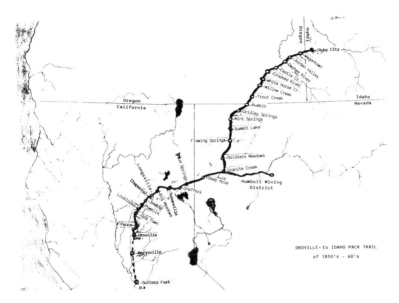

Oroville to Idaho Pack Trail of 1850s–1860s.

stopped to rest and water their weary animals. Occasionally a pack animal or ox would become lame or loose a shoe. The packers or immigrants would need to replace the lame animal in order to continue their journey.

Charles opened a blacksmith shop and kept a few extra head of mules, horses, and oxen at the station. He would trade animals, or shoe them, and sometimes repair wagons or harness. It soon became necessary for him to hire another man who understood blacksmithing and wagon repair.

Charles made it back to Susanville to help Maggie celebrate her twenty-seventh birthday on June 3, 1865. After catching up a few jobs around the farm that needed his attention, he put together some supplies and returned to the station.

On the Fourth of July 1865, Maggie with baby Harriet in her arms, and Jane and Tommy with little

Charlie in tow, went into town to watch the Honey Lake Rangers Parade, led by Dr. H.S. Borrette and his cornet band. The cavalry group proudly displayed the silk flag that the town ladies had made for them.

Seven days later on July 11, the first stage from Chico to Ruby City, Idaho, passed through Susanville. E.D. Pierce and J.B. Francis arranged with the stage stations along the route to stable relief teams, and to assist the drivers in changing teams. At Mud Spring Station it became the practice of Charles' wrangler to start harnessing up the relay team when he saw the stage, or the dust caused by it coming up the road, so passengers only had time to refresh themselves and wash down the dust with a cup of coffee or a shot of whiskey.

Near the middle of July, Major John Mullins, a well-known road builder, took over the management of the Chico-Idaho stage line. The following winter of 1865-66, he went to Washington, D.C. and with the help of Congressman John Bidwell, succeeded in getting a contract to carry the mail from Chico to Ruby City, for $45,000. He also got a pledge from the U.S. Army to provide the services of about two hundred soldiers along the route to protect the travelers from the robbers and Indian attacks that had plagued the stages and stations along the route the season before.

Early in 1866, a new stage company was formed with Major Mullins as president. With new financing, they sent J.R. Francis to Chico with cash to purchase five hundred head of horses and enough stagecoaches to stock the road. From then on the stage company began to provide its own teams and station its own wranglers at each relay station.

By July the new Concord Coaches and well-broken teams took only three days and five hours from Chico to Ruby City. Travelers bound for the Humboldt, Black

Rock, and Owyhee mining districts were all making relief stops at Mud Spring Station. Charles and his staff were kept busy tending the needs of the stage travelers, as well as the many freighters and their multi-horse and mule teams carrying supplies to the mining camps in Idaho, Montana and Nevada.

In August, Maggie learned she was again pregnant. Any thought of going to Chaparral House to pick up Alonzo was dashed. She was despondent with the knowledge that he was no doubt completely attached to the Philbrooks by now, and she would be a total stranger to her six-year-old son. Charles was still too occupied with his station to get away for such a long trip. Eliza's letters informing Maggie of the child's development and happiness did little to relieve her longing for him. Eliza's letters also indicated that business at the inn had dropped off considerably since the Chico-Humboldt road had become usable by stagecoaches. They were not sure the inn could continue to operate at a profit.

Maggie deeply regretted that she had not insisted on Alonzo coming with them when they came to Honey Lake Valley, regardless of the problems a four-year-old might have caused. Whenever Maggie was in town and a stage from Oroville was stopped there, she would search out the driver, and question him as to whether he had seen the boy at Chaparral House. She sought any information she could obtain concerning him. Some of the older drivers began to ask about him or to speak with him on their stops at Chaparral, and would leave what information they had obtained with the stage office for Maggie.

During the fall Maggie sent the Philbrooks her usual contribution for Alonzo's clothes. This year Eliza wrote not to worry. She said that Alonzo was doing fine, and that when they got back to Mud Creek she was going to enroll him in school at Chico. The letter did not relieve Maggie's yearning to see her child and have him a part of her family.

Her daughter Jane celebrated her twelfth birthday on New Years Day 1867. She was becoming quite a young lady: Maggie noticed that Jane was beginning to receive admiring glances from the single men when Jane accompanied her to town. Maggie cautioned Jane on the facts of life, and advised her to avoid any advances that might be made by men on her way to and from school or when she was in town by herself.

Compounding Maggie's problems and discomforts in the late stages of her pregnancy was the fact that twenty-three month old Harriet had begun to show signs of congestion. She was having respiratory problems and could hardly take nourishment. Dr. Z.N. Spalding medicated the small child to help her breathe.

On March 10, 1867, Maggie went into labor. Charles rushed to Dr. Spalding's home and summoned him to attend her. Charles, with Jane's help, took care of baby Harriet and little Charlie. Before the day was over Maggie gave birth to another baby girl. They named that child Mary Louisa Clark.

The family's joy over the arrival of the new baby was shattered ten days later. Little Harriet Eliza, no longer strong enough to overcome her sickness closed her eyes for the last time. Maggie was devastated by the loss of Harriet. Nothing since the death of Moses Oakes had so grievously affected her.

Still weak from giving birth to Mary Louisa, Maggie insisted that she accompany Charles and the children to the cemetery for the burial of little Harriet Eliza. Several of the town's housewives, sympathizing with Maggie, met them at the cemetery where the little girl was laid to rest with the recitation of the Lord's Prayer by the group. Only because she now had another infant girl that needed her loving care and attention, as well as older children who depended on her for their well being, was Maggie able to console herself.

Reports had been circulating in Susanville of problems with the Indians along the Humboldt and Idaho Road near the Nevada border. Collins Gaddy reported being shot at from ambush on his way back to Honey Lake Valley from the Black Rock mines. Reports came in of Indians running off cattle from Deep Hole Springs Station, and Charles Clark's wrangler reported seeing Indians prowling around Mud Flat near the station. A soldier with a scouting party near Summit Lake had been killed while standing guard duty. All these reports were extremely upsetting to Maggie. She was most apprehensive of Charles well being at Mud Spring Station and when enroute to or from the station.

Charles had experienced no problem with the Indians, and he felt Maggie was unduly concerned. However, in order to allay her fears, he agreed to spend more time at home and look for gainful employment in town.

He began to look for someone to buy Mud Spring Station. However, not many people were interested in settling down or investing in a business located close to the area where Indians had been causing so many problems. Charles finally talked the Chico and Idaho Stage Company into operating all but the trading post and eating house. He assigned more authority to his hired man and his wife, leaving them several days at a time to operate the post and cafe.

During the travel season of 1867, Charles spent more time on the farm with his family, giving consolation and support to Maggie. He assured her that they would eventually get into some venture in town that would allow them to be together the full time.

During the middle of August, Susanville residents were aroused to a frenzy when Paiute Chief

Winnemucca, accompanied by fifteen of his braves, came into Honey Lake Valley. Winnemucca stationed his braves on the foothills northeast of Susanville and, with one brave, rode into town looking for Isaac Roop. Winnemucca reportedly had letters from the Indian agent at their reservation and others, including one from Alvero Evans of Long Valley, written to Roop, requesting permission for the Indians to hunt in the hills surrounding the valley.

When the residents heard that Winnemucca was in town, a crowd of men began to gather around Isaac Roop and the Indians. Some valley residents had followed Winnemucca and his braves to town, and some of the town's residents who had gathered with their guns began to side with Joe Hale and Hank Wright, who were advocating they take the Indians and hang them. Isaac Roop told the group that he had smoked the peace pipe with the chief, and Winnemucca had always taken care of him. He told them they would have to kill him, before they hanged the Indians. Captain Weatherlow, William Hill Naileigh, John S. Ward, Cutler Arnold and some of the other prominent residents joined Roop, and kept the crowd back.

The Paiute brave that had accompanied Winnemucca to town was still mounted on his horse. He became nervous at the threatening group and took off down the road. Wright and some of the others mounted their horses and pursued him, but he outsmarted and outran them. The braves stationed north of town, seeing their companion running from the white men, scattered into the hills.

The officer in command of a small company of soldiers who were in Susanville at the time threatened to shoot any person who molested the Indians. This, of course, raised the tempers of those that had pursued the Indian. The townspeople and the soldiers spent some time quarreling among themselves. (The soldiers were one of several groups that had been stationed along the Humboldt and Idaho roads to protect the travelers. They did not want any action by the whites to arouse the hostility of the Indians.)

Isaac Roop meanwhile took Chief Winnemucca into his house for safekeeping. After a few days, when hostile feelings had cooled down, the soldiers escorted Winnemucca to Fort Bidwell, then released him to return to his reservation at Pyramid Lake.

Charles Clark had been an interested bystander during the chief's visit to town. His investment in Mud Spring Station could be wiped out at the will of the Paiute tribe. Being a relative newcomer to the valley, and unfamiliar with earlier conflicts, he chose not to take a partisan position.

Maggie feared that the Paiute braves might have returned to the reservation to get a war party to rescue their chief and retaliate against the settlers in the valley. She was somewhat relieved when Charles informed her the soldiers had escorted Winnemucca out of town. The Paiute braves had no doubt observed the chief in the company of the soldiers, and most likely followed, keeping him in sight.

A few weeks later, when Maggie was almost over her fear of an Indian attack on the town or Mud Spring Station, another blow fell. Word was received in Susanville that Charles League, on his way back to his home in Honey Lake Valley, had been ambushed and killed by renegade Pit River Indians on the morning of November 3, 1867, shortly after he left Flowing Springs Station near the Black Rock Desert in Nevada.

Alvaro Evans of Long Valley reported the killing to Chief Winnemucca. The chief with a party of twelve braves, along with a party of Long Valley settlers, tracked down the Pit River Indians.

# CHAPTER XI

## THE STEWARD HOUSE—1868-'70

Jane Oakes reached thirteen years of age on January 1, 1868. Tom Oakes turned twelve on February 12. And Alonzo Kelly, who was eight on April 1, and was still with the Philbrooks, a cause of great concern to Maggie. She had not seen the child in four years and had very little communication with the Philbrooks since early summer the year before. Eliza had not answered her letter sent in the fall. Although Maggie felt certain the Philbrooks would take good care of him, she made up her mind that she would definitely go to Chaparral House in the spring and bring Alonzo home with her.

When the first pack trains arrived from Oroville in April, Maggie quizzed the packers as to whether they had seen Alonzo. The first packer reported that Chaparral House had not open for business at the time he came by. Maggie began to experience strange feelings that things were not as they should be concerning Alonzo. When she mentioned her uneasiness to Charles, he reminded her the Philbrooks said they would enter Alonzo in school. He suggested that they might be waiting for the end of the school term before moving to the mountains.

Maggie's attention was again diverted to the problems the Pit River Indians were causing along the Humboldt Road. On April 4, 1868, Indians stole some of Charles' horses from Mud Spring Station. It was most unnerving to Maggie. Charles' loss was soon forgotten, however, when word reached Honey Lake Valley residents of the Massacre of the Pearson family on April 17, near Lower Hot Springs. The Pearsons were starting to move back to their home in Red Rock Valley in Nevada when they were ambushed and killed by renegade Pit River Indians. Rage and a terrifying fear gripped the valley.

A company of men was raised in Susanville under the command of A.A. Smith, captain of the Honey Lake Rangers, to search out and punish the murderers. They were joined the following day by others from Honey Lake Valley. They located the Indians' trail going north near Mud Spring Station. The following day they were joined by a group of Long Valley Settlers who had searched the area around Fort Sage Mountain. The Indians were nearly caught on several occasions, but they always managed to scatter among the rocks and brush. At the Pit River, the Indians succeeded in crossing the high water in the river and escaped.

Regular stage service from Oroville was resumed on May 1, 1868, and Maggie continued her practice of contacting the drivers for information about her son Alonzo. This year she was surprised and shocked to learn that the Philbrooks were not at Chaparral House. Another party was operating the Inn. As far as the drivers could learn, Alonzo Philbrook had not driven any livestock to the mountains.

Charles wrote letters to several of his former friends at Inskip. None seemed to know anything about the Philbrooks. Maggie tried writing to Eliza at Chico but got no response. She wrote to the public school at Chico asking about the boy Alonzo that the Philbrooks were supposed to have entered in school. She received a letter from the teacher stating that a seven-year-old boy called Alonzo Philbrook had been enrolled in the second grade the past school term, but they had no information on his present whereabouts. They thought he might return when school resumed in the fall.

Except for the Honey Lake Rangers, Charles Clark had not been a joiner. However, after the Silver Star Lodge No. 135 Independent Order of Odd Fellows was chartered in Susanville on June 19, 1868, his friends Dr. Spalding, Samuel Peyser, and David Knoch, who were charter members, prevailed upon him and several other prominent Susanville residents to join the fraternal order. Charles B. Clark became one of the .first initiates to be taken into the new lodge.

The Steward House Hotel in Susanville, Lassen County, California (built 1864). Photo courtesy Lassen Historical Society, Susanville, California.

During the summer Charles disposed of his interest in Mud Spring Station. He began to spend his full time at home on the farm while searching for a business venture in Susanville. He and Maggie were both greatly relieved that they were no longer involved with the station-especially when, in September, they learned that an employee of stockman J.R. Witherington, driving cattle from Mud Flat, had been attacked by Indians.

During the fall, Charles learned that Samuel Johnston, the proprietor of the Steward House Hotel, was going to give up his lease, and the owners Miller and Kingsley were looking for someone to operate the hotel, bar and dining room. Charles told Maggie about this. She at once became interested. Her years of experience working in boarding houses led her to believe that together they could successfully operate Susanville's largest and most prestigious hotel. They discussed the pros and cons of the hotel business, and decided to meet with Miller and Kingsley to determine what kind of a deal might be worked out.

Maggie proposed to handle the kitchen, dining room and chambermaid work. Charles would man the bar, stage office, and many other business-related activities. Jane and Tom were both getting old enough to help out, after school and on weekends, with the lighter chores. Young Charlie would be starting school next year, and he would not be a problem. Maggie was sure she could manage the care of little Mary Louisa.

Charles met with Miller and Kingsley at their store in the hotel building, and worked out a deal to take over the hotel in December 1868. The Clarks moved to the Steward House on December 1, and the local paper, the *Sage Brush*, printed the following article on December 19, 1868.

> Mr. C.B. Clark has assumed the proprietorship of the Steward House, and is now in full blast. He proposes to do the clean thing by all who choose to patronize him.
> Hear all ye that are hungry and dry; come in

eat and drink.
Board—per week .................. $7.00
Board with lodging .............. $8.00

December was a quiet time of the year for the hotel as the stages and most of the packers discontinued travel for the winter months. Maggie and Charles began to cater to the local clientele and were soon doing a good business in the saloon and dining room. On New Year's Eve they held a ball which turned out to be a great success. The price per couple was $5.00, which included a delicious midnight buffet prepared by Maggie. She was assisted in serving by her daughter Jane, who had enjoyed dancing with the younger men in attendance. On January 1, 1869, Maggie served a delicious New Year's Day dinner for the regular boarders and several local couples. The family observed Jane's fourteenth birthday with a large cake that was shared with all the diners.

Charles negotiated a deal with Sheriff T.N. Long to feed the prisoners that were confined in the jail. When the sheriff had someone in custody, Charles would carry a tray of food to the jail once a day.

Tom Oakes observed his thirteenth birthday on February 12, 1869. He had become a well-developed young lad and was beginning to be quite helpful around the hotel. His main chore was to keep the wood boxes full for the stoves in the kitchen, lobby and saloon. That was no small chore during the winter months, when warming fires were needed day and night.

February 14, 1869, was a day of sorrow in Susanville. Isaac N. Roop, the first white settler in Honey Lake Valley and founder of the town named for his daughter Susan, died at the age of forty-seven. There were few people living in Susanville at that time whose lives had not been touched in some way by his helpful

Advertisement by C.B. Clark for Steward House Hotel in December 19, 1868, *Lassen Advocate*.

and generous acts. His efforts to bring law and order to the area had made him a true and trusted friend to whites and Indians alike. He was buried with Masonic honors in the cemetery he had generously donated to the town he established.

In February, Charles Clark advertised a gala Washington's Birthday Ball at the Steward House for the night of February 22nd. The ball was a pleasant social event for the town's residents, who welcomed the opportunity to get together and socialize after having been housebound during the winter months.

Little Mary Louisa's second birthday was observed by the family on March 10. She had become the darling of Steward House, as the travelers and regular boarders stopped to admire her, much to Maggie's delight. The little girl was in good health and showed every sign of growing into a beautiful young lady. Much of Jane's time, when not in school, was spent helping care for Mary Louisa, and assisting her mother serving the meals.

Word of the discovery of gold at Hayden Hill, some forty miles north of Susanville, began to attract miners and prospectors from California and Nevada. Many of them stopped at the Steward House overnight, or until they could arrange transportation to the new discovery area. This provided a welcome boost to the hotel business after a slow winter, when travel was at a near standstill.

When the stages started arriving from Oroville, Maggie again questioned everyone she thought might have some information on the Philbrooks' whereabouts. From some of the Chico travelers, she learned the Philbrooks had disposed of their property on Mud Creek and left the country. For the next few months she continued to question all the passengers from Chico, but none were able to provide any helpful information.

Maggie and Charles observed their seventh anniversary quietly on April 23, 1869. Two days later, on young Charlie's sixth birthday, Maggie hosted a party at the hotel. She invited all the town's children who were about his age, and their mothers. The small guests played games while the mothers spent the afternoon visiting. A large cake was cut and served to everyone after the six candles had been blown out with help from several of the children present.

Time passed rapidly, with new travelers arriving and departing on the various stages. Before Maggie realized it, Charles was presenting her with a gift for her thirty-first birthday. A month later the Lassen County Assessor, Charles Cramer, appointed Charles Clark his deputy. Early that fall, Charles announced his candidacy for the office of Justice of the Peace, citing his experience as Justice of Kimhew Township in Butte County. At a special election held on October 12, 1869, Charles was elected, along with H.K. Cornell, as Justice of the Peace for the Susanville district.

Travel began to slow down around the middle of November. In order to stimulate business for the Steward House, Charles began to advertise a Christmas Eve Ball, with tickets at $4.00. Maggie and Charles were quite busy for several days before the ball with the last minute preparations: decorating the ballroom, preparing the refreshments, and getting in a big supply of wood to keep the heating stoves in the lobby and ballroom well fueled until the early hours of Christmas day.

The ball was well attended and successful. The revelers danced until the early hours of the morning. It was well after 4.00 A.M. when Charles and Maggie were able to retire for some badly needed rest.

On Christmas morning, Maggie was surprised to find that Charles was still in bed, and the fires had not been stoked. She tried to wake him but was unable to arouse him. On close examination she realized he was not breathing. Panic stricken, she screamed for Jane who, along with Tom, was already up and dressed in anticipation of Christmas morning. They both ran into the bedroom and Maggie told Jane to go to Dr. Spalding's residence and tell him to come at once. Something was wrong with Charles.

Dr. Spalding arrived a short time later, and upon examination told Maggie that Charles' heart had apparently stopped beating during his sleep. It appeared Charles had overtaxed his heart during the preparations for the Christmas ball, and the long exhausting hours looking after the needs of the dancers.

Maggie was devastated by the sudden demise of the man she had so loved and admired. The man with whom she had shared her bed for nearly eight years and with whom she had expected to spend the rest of her life, sharing every confidence, joy and sorrow.

In spite of her grief, there were regular boarders at the Steward House requiring regular meals. They had been promised a special Christmas Day meal. Fortunately, Maggie had most of the Christmas dinner planned well ahead. All the necessary preparations had been made. With the help of Jane and Tom, she managed to cook the turkey and other dishes and to serve the boarders. Maggie had baked pumpkin pies the day before. The boarders were greatly saddened by Charles' death, and expressed their sympathy to Maggie. Even though everyone was well-fed, the atmosphere at the Steward House that Christmas was one of profound sorrow, as it was about town when the word spread of Charles' sudden death.

The following day funeral services were held in the Steward House Hall. The members of Silver Star Lodge No. 135 I.O.O.F. conducted memorial services and escorted the body to the cemetery, where thirty-nine-year-old Charles B. Clark was laid to rest beside his infant daughter Harriet Eliza. Appropriate music was provided by the Susanville Cornet Band, directed by Dr. H.S. Borrette.

At the December 30 meeting of the Silver Star Lodge No. 135 I.O.O.F. the following resolution was unanimously adopted.

> Whereas, It having pleased an all-wise Providence to remove from us by death, our beloved brother C.B. Clark,
>
> Therefore, Resolved, That we tender our sincere and heartfelt sympathy to the family and friends of our late brother in their sad bereavement, and earnestly point them to Him, who in His infinite wisdom "Doeth all things well".
>
> Resolved, That in respect to the memory of our brother, the members wear the usual badge of mourning thirty days.
>
> Resolved, That the forgoing Preamble and Resolution be entered in full upon the records of the lodge, a copy under the seal of the lodge be presented to the widow of our deceased brother, and a copy furnished to the *Sage Brush* for publication.
>
> J.S. Ward
> Z.N. Spalding          Committee
> E.P. Soule

Maggie and Charles had worked together very closely in operating the Steward House. Maggie had an understanding of the business end of the operation, so she was able to continue the business by hiring a bartender, and employing Indians part time to split and stack the wood.

Jane turned fifteen on New Year's Day 1870. She

now became a full-time assistant to her mother in the kitchen and dining room. Maggie continued to manage the Steward House through March 1870. At that time Mrs. C.T. Emerson leased the hotel and took over the management.

Maggie was in a relatively comfortable situation financially. Charles Clark's business acumen and conservative nature had left her moderately well off. With few options open to her, Maggie planned to remain in Susanville, at least until Charlie and Mary Louisa had finished school. In order to conserve her finances, Maggie made an arrangement with Mrs. Emerson to continue operating the Steward House dining room, with Jane's help, preparing meals and waiting on tables, and Tom carrying in the wood for the kitchen stove. They were able to continue a good rapport with the regular boarders, as well as with the travelers and other occasional patrons, all of whom seemed to enjoy the big family atmosphere.

Among the regular boarders at Maggie's table were the Honorable Judge John S. Chapman, and his younger brother Francis Sprig Chapman, a thirty-one year old deputy county clerk. The Chapman brothers, accompanied by their two sisters, had come to California from Arkansas in 1859. John had served as Lassen County clerk from 1866 until he had been elected county judge in 1869.

Francis Sprig Chapman and Dr. John A. Slater had erected a hewn-log building near Janesville during the fall of 1859. That building later served as a fort in the 1860 Indian Uprising, and became known as Fort Janesville.

Francis S. Chapman, after a few months at Maggie Clark's table, became enamored with the sprightly fifteen-year-old Jane Minerva Oakes, as she flitted about the room waiting on the boarders. Jane soon became aware of the admiring glances she was receiving from the attractive gentleman, some fifteen years her senior. At first she was flattered by the unexpected attention, and began to return the glances with a smile. Not many weeks passed before Francis Chapman began to stall around after the evening meal to engage Jane in casual conversation.

When Jane's friendly chats with Francis became so frequent and lengthy that they delayed clearing the table and washing the dishes, Maggie began quizzing Jane about her feelings for Francis. She learned that Jane had become highly infatuated with him, and cautioned her daughter that she was too young to become involved with any man, especially one so many years older than herself. Jane was quick to remind her mother that she was fifteen when she married her father, Moses Oakes, and that Maggie did not then consider it too young.

Realizing that Jane was becoming serious in her feelings toward Francis, Maggie confronted him as to his intentions. She was surprised to learn that he had developed a serious attraction to Jane. He made it clear that he would very much like to marry Jane, provided Maggie gave her consent, and if Jane was willing to make a lifetime commitment to him. Maggie told Francis she wanted what was best for Jane and that the final decision was hers to make.

When Maggie related to Jane the conversation she had with Francis Chapman, she cautioned her daughter to be positive that she was ready for such a commitment before rushing into marriage. Maggie recounted for Jane the many problems she had encountered in her marriages, and how she had been left alone to raise small children. Maggie pleaded with her to take more time and consider all the aspects of married life before making a final decision, and if she was sure, to wait until she turned sixteen to speak her vows.

The Francis Sprig Chapman-Jane Minerva Oakes courtship continued through the holiday season of 1870. Shortly thereafter they were joined in matrimony by the groom's brother Judge John S. Chapman, in the presence of Maggie, her children, the groom's sisters and husbands, Mr. and Mrs. A.A. Smith, and Mr. and Mrs. F.A. Sloss.

# CHAPTER XIII

## GEORGE W. GREENO

Among the Honey Lake and Long Valley ranchers who had enjoyed Maggie Clark's New England style cuisine at the Steward House was George W. Greeno, a bachelor pioneer stockman from Long Valley.

George Greeno was among the first settlers in what became known as Long Valley, in Lassen County, California, situated along the Nevada border.

He was a native of Norfork, Virginia, born in April 1816. When he was nine years old his family sent him to England to attend school. After completing his education at the age of nineteen, he went to sea, sailing behind the mast for fifteen years.

Landing in California in 1850, following the discovery of gold, he decided to abandon the sea and try his luck in the gold fields. He mined along the Yuba River for three years. In 1854 he went to Plumas County, where he built the Mountain House, a stopping place on the pack trail between Spanish Ranch and Rich Bar. In 1857, he packed over the mountains to Honey Lake Valley and into Long Valley, in search of a place to settle and put down roots. Two years later, at the age of forty-three, he returned to Lassen County and claimed 160 acres of land at the lower end of Long Valley. The following year he built a cabin on his claim, and began raising livestock, grazing the herd on the vast open rangelands east of Honey Lake, and in the mountains along the Nevada boundary and westward into Plumas County.

Like other pioneer settlers in the area, he participated in the early Indian wars to protect his livestock
and property. During June of 1860, his first year in the
valley, he rode with his neighbor John Byrd and his
company in pursuit of Indians, following the Major
Ormsby massacre in the Pyramid Lake area. In March
1862, he again joined his friend John Byrd in pursuit of
the Indians that had driven off cattle grazing in Honey
Lake Valley. During the last part of October 1862, he
joined in pursuit of Indians that had attacked immigrants near Shaffer's ranch and a group of prospectors
returning from the Humboldt mines killing two of the
miners and wounding three others. In April 1868,
George Greeno was among the company of twenty-five
Long Valley residents who accompanied Newt and
Alvaro Evans in their search and pursuit of the Indians
that had massacred the Pearson family and S.C. Cooper.

On his occasional trips to Susanville, George
Greeno became attracted to Maggie Clark's striking
good looks, her vivacious personality, her interesting
New England accent, and her delicious food. After
Charles Clark's death, George Greeno always stopped
at the Steward House for meals when in Susanville. He
made it a point to personally compliment Maggie on the
meal and engage her in conversation.

By the summer of 1871, George Greeno's trips to
Susanville became more frequent. He began to bring
Maggie small gifts he had purchased in Reno or Virginia
City, in appreciation, he claimed, for the delicious food
she served. The gifts continued to come everytime
George Greeno stopped by for a meal.

Taking his attention more seriously, Maggie began
to extract more information of a personal nature from
the fifty-five year old ex-seaman-turned-cattleman. Although he was twenty-two years her senior, the fact
that he had spent many years at sea, and the experi-

ences he told, reminded her of the stories Moses Oakes and Josiah West related back in Boston. As a result, she began to sense a kindred spirit in the attentive Southerner.

During the summer, Maggie learned her daughter Jane, called "Jennie" by her husband, was pregnant. The thought of becoming a grandmother at the age of thirty-three was a sobering experience for Maggie. She had always looked upon grandmothers as middle-aged or older.

The thought of a new baby in the family reminded her more acutely of the child she had left in the custody of the Philbrooks. He would now be a boy of eleven, whom she had not seen or held in her arms since he was four. Unable to locate either the child or the Philbrooks, her heart ached as she silently cursed herself for having left him in their care. The only redeeming fact was her knowledge that they loved Alonzo dearly and were undoubtedly taking good care of him.

During the late summer, Francis Chapman announced his intention to run for the office of county clerk. At the September election he received 226 votes while his opponent received 206. Maggie was greatly pleased that the majority of county voters had looked favorably upon her son-in-law, assuring him and Jennie a steady income.

As fall approached in 1871, George Greeno finished putting up hay stacks for the winter feeding of his horses and milk cow. He then began to spend more time in Susanville, pursuing Maggie. There was no doubt that he was attracted to her. He often told his neighbors and friends that he was seeing the prettiest woman in Susanville. He finally got around to proposing to Maggie, telling her he realized that he was considerably older, but that he was doing quite well in the livestock business, and could offer a home for her and the children.

Maggie was flattered by George Greeno's proposal, but no one could replace Charles Clark whom she had dearly loved and admired. She was reluctant to step into another relationship, but George's persistence was hard to resist. The idea of a home on a cattle ranch intrigued her. She had been interested in raising livestock since her association with Alonzo Philbrook and the other cattlemen who drove their stock past the Chaparral House. She thought it would be a good business for her two sons to learn.

Maggie finally capitulated and agreed to marry George, but only after her daughter Jennie had her baby. Maggie wanted to be available to help Jennie during and after the birth of her first child.

On November 13, 1871, Maggie became a grandmother, when Jennie Chapman gave birth to a baby daughter they named Evalina Chapman.

News of the birth of Maggie's granddaughter brought joy to George Greeno, the tough old seaman turned stockman. He immediately rode to Susanville and reminded Maggie of her promise to marry him.

Maggie, in preparing for her wedding, gave up the dining room at the Steward House. She made arrangements for young Charlie Clark to stay in Susanville with the Chapmans until the end of the school term.

On November 22, 1871, Margaret Ann "Maggie" Clark and George W. Greeno were united in marriage by the Honorable County Judge, John S. Chapman. In attendance at the wedding were Maggie's daughter Jennie, sons Tom Oakes and Charlie Clark, her young daughter Mary Louisa Clark and son-in-law Francis Chapman. The Saturday, November 25, 1871, issue of the *Sage Brush* printed the following notice.

Married: In Susanville Nov. 22nd by Hon. J.S. Chapman County Judge, Mr. George Greeno of Long Valley, to Mrs. Maggie Clark of Susanville.

The printer being recipients of a liberal share of Champagne, drank sundry bumpers to the health and happiness of the newly wedded pair.

Maggie's move to the ranch in Long Valley was a letdown. The accommodations were less than what she had been accustomed to. She had expected the ranch house to be large, but instead it was hardly more than a two-room cabin to which Greeno had tacked on two rough rooms and a screened porch in the back. The house sat on the side of a sagebrush hill that separated Long Valley from Honey Lake Valley. There were no trees to provide shade or break the desert winds. The inside of the house was harsh and unfriendly. The walls were unpainted and the floors were rough planks with no coverings.

Maggie hid her disappointment and began to plan how she would make it more livable. She would add a feminine touch and when spring came she would see to it that some trees were planted.

When Maggie approached George about fixing the house, he told her that he thought it was just fine the way it was. He saw no reason to spend good money on such things as lace curtains, table linens, or rugs. Needless to say, the marriage got off to a rough start. The Boston-raised, family-oriented, thirty-three-year-old Yankee and the Virginia-bred bachelor found their ideas of marriage did not conform with each other.

George, who had been accustomed to living alone, was annoyed by the children. He was especially annoyed by Tom, who was nearly sixteen, curious to learn about ranch life, and who kept plying George with questions. Tom also did not always perform his assigned chores as promptly as George believed he should. This led to disagreements where Maggie found herself in the middle, trying to appease the old seaman and the young lad.

A major disagreement occurred during the holidays. Maggie's eight-year-old son, Charlie, came to stay during the school vacation, and without asking George, Maggie invited her daughter Jennie and family to spend Christmas with them. The small ranch house was quite crowded as the family gathered around the dinner table. George annoyed by the children made snide remarks about having to feed the whole tribe.

Tom Oakes was quick to decide that he would never get along with his new step-father, and he asked his sister Jennie if he could return to Susanville and stay with them. Jennie and her husband agreed that he was welcome. Francis Chapman recognized that things where not going smoothly between George and Maggie, and he told her she and the children were welcome to come and stay with them, if she so desired.

Maggie and George continued to disagree on many things, especially things that pertained to the children, even after Charlie and Tom had returned to Susanville with the Chapmans. Little Mary Louisa, whom George seemed to take a liking to, remained with her mother. Each time Maggie asked for some item for herself or Mary Louisa, an argument ensued.

Things came to a head in March 1872, when Maggie asked George to pick up a small gift for Mary Louisa's fifth birthday, and he protested about her frivolous ways with money. It was then that she came to the conclusion that the marriage was not going to work out. She decided she could no longer live with his tight-fisted ways. She had funds of her own and would find some way of making a living and support her children.

Maggie told George she would no longer put up with his actions and intended to leave. George thought she was bluffing, that she would not dare leave him. He believed a wife should be subservient to her husband. When the Susanville stage came by the Greeno house on March 23,1872, Maggie and Mary Louisa were waiting beside the road with their bags. Maggie hailed the stage to stop.

George was out in the pasture on his horse checking on the early spring grass. From a distance he saw the stage stop at his house, and thinking the driver was leaving off mail, he started back toward the house. He had not gone far when he noticed the stage driver loading Maggie's luggage on top of the coach. He spurred his horse to a gallop but the stage departed before he reached the road.

In a rage, he hitched up his horse and buggy and started out after the stage. By that time it had a several-mile head start on him. Even though the stage made short stops to deliver mail at Milford and Janesville, George Greeno never caught up with it until they reached the Steward House in Susanville.

George confronted Maggie on the porch of the Steward House as she was retrieving her bags. She was glad there were several witnesses standing on the porch waiting for the driver to unload the stage, as she could see that George was really angry and might have otherwise become abusive. She refused to listen to his demand that she return to the ranch, and informed him she intended to take legal action against him. Then she picked up her bags, called Mary Louisa to come along, and headed for Jennie's home.

George Greeno's wrath prompted him to walk up

the street to the *Sage Brush* office and place the following notice in the paper.

### NOTICE

My wife Maggie Greeno having this day left
my bed and board without just cause or provoca-
tion; I hereby forbid any person trusting her on
my account. I will pay no debts of her contract-
ing.

Dated at Long Valley
Lassen County, Cal.
March 23, 1872.
Signed
George Greeno.

Maggie continued to stay with Jennie for the next
several weeks, during which time George Greeno made
several trips to Susanville in an effort to persuade her
to return to his ranch. After considering the legal com-
plications his marriage might have upon his property
and business dealings, he finally persuaded Maggie to
consent to the following agreement.

AGREEMENT: Between George Greeno
first party, and Maggie Greeno wife, second
party. April 25, 1872.

That in consequence of various unhappy dif-
ferences which have arisen between the said
parties they have agreed to live separate and
apart from each other during the remainder of
their lives, and the said party of the first part in
consideration of the premises and the covenants
and conditions of the said party of the second
part, hereinafter

Enumerated: covenants and agrees to and
with the said party of the second part, that she

the said party of the second part may live separate and apart from the said party of the first
part, at such place and with such families relatives or: friends as she may deem fit, without
hindrances or molestation from or by the said
party of the first part, and the said party of the
first part further covenants and agrees to and
with said party of the second part that he will
pay her upon the execution of these presents the
sum of ($300.00) in gold coin, and in addition
thereto will give to the said party of the second
part one "Florence" sewing machine, and the
party of the first part further covenants and
agrees to and with the said party of the second
part. That upon the execution of these presents
he will make, execute, stamp and deliver to the
said party of the second part two promissory
notes, one for the sum of ($200.00) in gold coin
payable one day after date. One for the sum of
($200.00) in gold coin payable on or before the
first day of October A.D. 1872. The sum of
money to be paid as herein before mentioned for
the sole and separate use of the said party of the
second part to be used and expended by her in
any manner she may deem with, and said party
of the second part in consideration of the covenants and conditions herein before mentioned,
covenants and agrees to and with the said party
of the first part that she will accept the sewing
machine and sums of money hereinafter mentioned at the times aforesaid, and will hold the
said party of the first part harmless and exempt
from any future debts claims or demand for or
on account of the support and maintenance of
said party of the second part so long as the parties shall continue to live separate, and the party

of the second part convenants and agrees to and with the said party of the first part that she will not call upon nor suffer any other to call upon the said party of the first part for any sum of money, debt, claims or demand for or on account of the maintenance or support of the said party of the second part, and the parties further convenant and agree to and with each other that they will mutually refrain from any injury one to the other. The said party of the second part further convenants and agrees she will sign any deed or deeds, bills of sale, or other assurances to which her signature may be necessary to enable the party of the first part to dispose of any property which he may now have or in which the party of the second part may have an interest whenever such deed, bill of sale, or other assurance may be presented to her for such purpose.

In Witness whereof, the said parties have hereunto set their hands and seals the day and year first above written.

George Greeno
Maggie Greeno
Witnessed by, F.S. Chapman County Clerk.
Recorded by George Greeno, April 25th, 1872. Book B. Page 294.

George Greeno was aware that Maggie was pregnant with his child at the time they executed the agreement. He continued to plead with her to reconsider and move back to the ranch. George finally promised Maggie that she could have full say of the house and children, and he would comply with her wishes and listen to her suggestions.

Finally, convinced that George meant what he promised, Maggie agreed to return to the ranch, with the understanding she would immediately leave if he reverted to his previous manner and demands.

Back on the Long Valley ranch, Maggie noted that the rough, tough old cattleman was trying very hard to mend his manner and assume the ways of a family man. He took a fatherly attitude toward young Charlie and Mary Louisa. He taught nine-year-old Charlie to ride a horse, toss a lasso, and the basic techniques of herding cattle.

On September 23, 1872, Maggie gave birth to twin boys. Unfortunately one twin was very weak and survived only a few hours. The surviving boy was named George W. Greeno, Jr. after his father. He would later be called "G." The birth of his son had a sobering effect on George Greeno. He developed a more compassionate attitude toward Maggie and the children. He even became more tolerant of Maggie's questions about his cattle business and his methods of operation. He also endeavored to become more socially inclined toward Magqie's relatives and friends. He made no objections when Maggie wished to visit and become better acquainted with her neighbors in Long Valley, and he invited them to stop by for a visit.

On their first wedding anniversary, November 22, 1872, he even gave Maggie her own horse, broken both for side-saddle and buggy. He encouraged her to utilize the buggy to visit the neighbor ladies, and to take part in their sewing bees and social get-togethers.

There being no school in Long Valley at that time, Maggie sent Charlie Clark back to Susanville to stay with Jennie during the school term. She tutored six-year-old Mary Louisa in basic reading, writing and arithmetic. The care of baby George, housekeeping chores, sewing and mending clothing occupied most of Maggie's days. She found little time to visit neighbors who lived from one to ten miles away, except on the occasions when they needed help with the birth of a child, or some serious illness in the family. In those circumstances she always managed to go and assist the families.

In June 1873, Maggie traveled to Susanville to assist Jennie with the birth of her second child, a baby girl they named Maggy Bell Chapman in honor of her grandmother.

At the county election held in September, Francis Chapman lost his bid for re-election. When his term expired, the family moved north to the town of Alturas in Modoc County. There he associated with D.C. Slater in the publication of a small newspaper known as the *Modoc Independent.*

Maggie continued to observe and learn the methods George Greeno used in the operation of his livestock business. George was accustomed to being his own man. He was not as prone to discuss his financial dealings, or confide his thoughts and problems with Maggie, as Charles Clark had been. She was able to discreetly pump the information she desired out of George, and in that manner soon gained an understanding of his methods of raising and selling cattle.

Early in the spring of 1874, Maggie became pregnant for the eighth time. George Greeno was quite proud of the fact that at fifty-eight-years of age he had sired another child. He bragged to the neighboring ranchers of his manly ability, sometimes even chiding the younger married men who had not fathered children. On September 15, 1874, Maggie gave birth to a baby girl whom they named Anna Francis Greeno.

By Maggie and George's third wedding anniversary in November, they had reconciled themselves to each other's idiosyncrasies, and were living a near normal family life. Maggie, by that time, had gained a full understanding of George's ranching methods. She found him willing to discuss suggestions and ideas she would occasionally put forth.

There were many things about George's cattle-raising methods that bothered Maggie. First and foremost was the fact that he never knew for sure how many cattle he had or where they were. Like all livestockmen in that area, he turned his stock loose to graze on the desert year round. Twice a year the stockmen would get together and hold a rodeo (roundup), during which they would fan out on horseback across the desert, and drive all the livestock they found toward one roundup point. There they would separate the stock according to their brands. Each rancher would cut out his prime stock that was ready for sale. They would brand the new calves or colts with the owner's registered brand, and then turn them, with the stock they did not wish to sell, loose again to forage on the desert grass and brush until the next rodeo.

Maggie was also concerned that with more settlers getting into the livestock business, the desert was becoming overpopulated with livestock, and overgrazing the land would eventually reduce the amount of feed available, limiting the number of cattle the ranchers could raise. She had observed that those ranchers who had larger areas of meadowland along the creek were able to cut sizable crops of hay. During the winter months they fed their calf-heavy cows and young steers from the summer hay stacks. That eliminated a great amount of stock loss during the winter. She also noted those ranchers who had hay to feed their market stock had fatter, better-conditioned cattle to sell. Maggie began to talk George into the idea that he should try to find some meadowland where he could cut more hay to feed his cattle, instead of just enough for the ranch horses and milk cow.

The year 1875 created some additional obstacles for

the original livestockmen of the area. On March 3, the United States Congress passed the Desert Land Act. The Act allowed individuals to claim up to 640 acres of desert land. Many individuals began to file claims on land the stockmen had freely grazed their stock upon. In order to protect himself, George Greeno filed a declaratory statement with the U.S. Land Office on May 15, 1875, for a claim covering his ranch property.

Maggie went to Susanville in June to see her daughter Jennie and her grandchildren, who had returned from Modoc County. Francis Chapman had sold his interest in the *Modoc Independent* and accepted a position in the Lassen County School Superintendent's Office.

Maggie's son, nineteen-year-old Tom Oakes, was an apprentice in the cabinet and furniture shop of George W. Harrison. He had been supporting himself for nearly two years. When his sister Jennie asked him to move in with them, he readily accepted.

On August 22, 1875, Jennie gave birth to her third child, a baby girl they named Edna. Maggie was there to assist Jennie during the birth.

When George Greeno drove his cattle to Reno that fall, he was disappointed to find the price of beef low, and he received less than he had hoped for. Hard times had fallen on the whole country. Those needing to borrow money with which to operate were finding financing tight. Fortunately, the Greenos did not need to borrow; because of George's conservative nature, he had avoided going in debt.

Problems for the stockmen compounded during the winter. In January 1876, blizzards left two-and-a-half feet of snow on the ground in Honey Lake and Long Valley. Cattle on the range were unable to get feed and many succumbed to the cold temperature.

On the spring rodeo, the stockmen found the carcasses of several hundred head of cattle scattered over the desert. The severe winter had depleted their herds to a far greater extent than they had anticipated. George Greeno's herd was no exception. At branding time he found the winter had been especially hard on the young stock, and it would take him several seasons to rebuild the herd. The cattle that had survived the winter were in too poor a condition to offer for sale. It was fall before some of the herd had put on enough weight to become market grade beef.

When Maggie learned the extent to which the cattle had suffered during the winter storms, she became convinced that some changes had to he made in their operating methods. When she discussed the matter with George, he agreed that getting feed from beneath the snow was a serious problem for the cattle, but he was at a loss to figure out a solution as the herd was scattered over miles of open range.

George traveled to Susanville each fall to pay his county taxes and to transact any other business he might have pending. Maggie and the children usually accompanied him, and while he tended to business, she visited Jennie and Tom and her Susanville friends. The trip also provided her with the opportunity to shop for material to make clothes for the family and to buy other items needed at the ranch. She never failed to contact the Chico and Oroville stage drivers and any other persons she thought might have information on the whereabouts of the Philbrooks and her son Alonzo. Her letters to the Chico school and the Butte County Sheriff had been of little help.

# CHAPTER XIV

## LONG VALLEY

The winter of 1876-1877 in Long Valley was relative mild. The livestock had no problem getting to the bunch grass that grew around the sage brush. There was a good calf crop and the beef cattle came through in top shape.

Young Charlie Clark, now fourteen, was beginning to be a big help with the livestock. He was participating in the spring and fall rodeos, and helping with the branding and the cattle drives. That spring when the Greeno herd was driven to Reno for shipment to market, Charlie was one of the drovers.

Maggie's observation of the effects of winter on the herds convinced her that in order to maintain good prime beef herds, it was absolutely necessary for the cattle to get a steady supply of feed during the winter months. She began to expound her theory to George, and urged him to try and acquire additional meadow-land upon which they could harvest a larger crop of hay for winter feed, and also have better winter pasture for the cows and calves.

The following winter, Maggie learned that the ranch up the road from theirs, which was mostly meadow-land, was for sale. George tried to make a deal for the ranch, but he and the owner were unable to come to an equitable agreement. Maggie was disappointed, but it later became known that several of the land owners further up Long Valley Creek were arguing over the use of water. Notice was served on Edwin Dunning, Joseph Williams, and Albert E. Ross in an attempt to stop them from diverting water from the creek, which would have a serious effect on the meadows in the lower end of the valley. George thought it best to await the outcome of the dispute before trying to purchase any property along the creek.

In the meantime, Rueben Chamberlin purchased the property next to theirs in March 1878. He immediately set about making improvements with the view in mind of establishing a stage stop with meals for the passengers.

Later in the year, Chamberlin built a large corral with a high, strong fence to hold the wild range cattle

Barn and corral (built 1878) at Chamberlin Station Ranch. Photo by McDow 1991.

being driven to Reno. He planned to sell feed for the livestock, and to supply lodging as well as meals for the drovers.

Maggie became friends with Mrs. Chamberlin who had two small children and was expecting another. When her time came to give birth on September 29, 1878, Maggie was there to give her assistance.

In October, George took his entire family to Susanville for the first annual fair of the Plumas, Lassen and Modoc District Fair Association. He looked after business affairs while in town, and attended the horse races and livestock exhibits. Maggie visited with friends and spent part of one day viewing the domestic exhibits. Jennie and her family had moved to Oregon, where Francis had taken a position with the Lake County School Superintendent. That year the Greeno family was obliged to stay at the Steward House.

In February the following year, Mr. J.M. Steinberger traded his flour mill at Milford, in Honey Lake Valley, to Hiram Dakin for his Willow Ranch, about five miles up the valley from Greeno's. It was a ranch that Maggie and George would have liked very much to own, but Steinberger's flour mill was more attractive to Dakin than anything the Greenos had to offer.

On July 1, 1879, George was hitching his team to the mowing machine when something spooked his horses. Six-year-old George Jr. was nearly run over by the stampeding horses. The horses continued up the road with the mowing machine. At Mr. Chamberlin's place he, his young son, and Samuel Cashman avoided being cut down by running to the side of the road. in passing Chamberlin's new corral, the mowing machine struck a post and was completely destroyed. The terrified animals ran for six miles before they were caught. Harvesting that season was delayed several days until Greeno's could find another mowing machine.

The second annual District Fair, held in Susanville October 27, through October 31, 1879, brought many ranchers to town. Among them was George Greeno and his family. While in town they visited friends, and Maggie's son Tom Oakes, who was then employed full time in Harrison's cabinet shop.

The winter of 1879-1880 turned out to be another

severe one for the livestock. Waterholes and creeks froze over and the ground was covered with snow. In late December. a severe storm struck. George Greeno and several other stockmen made an effort to roundup as many beef cattle as the freezing weather would permit, and drove them to Reno stock yards for feeding.

The range cattle were scattered over such an enormous area that time and the stormy weather did not allow them to search out a large part of their herds. George and young Charlie Clark spent several cold hard days in the saddle, searching the windswept, snow-covered desert. They succeeded in rounding up about a hundred more beeves for market.

The early spring rodeo revealed the cattlemen had suffered a substantial loss of livestock, and the Greenos' herd was no exception. During the latter part of March, several Honey Lake Valley cattlemen drove their herds passed the Greeno ranch on the way to Reno. On their return, the drovers stopped at Greenos' and reported the market was flooded with cattle purchased from Honey Lake and Long Valley ranchers in January by Garrick, Hays and Company of Oakland. Due to that fact, and the poor condition of the steers, the price had dropped.

Among the returning cattlemen was Maggie's brother, William "Bill" West, who had moved to Honey Lake Valley and was working for James D. Byers, Lassen County's largest livestock rancher. Bill always stopped by the Greeno ranch to visit Maggie whenever a rodeo or cattle drive brought him near Long Valley.

The residents of Long Valley were excited about the possibility of railroad service becoming available in their area. In June 1880, John T. Davis and Colonel Moore organized The Nevada and Oregon Railroad Company, and proposed to build a railroad from Reno through Long Valley and on to Oregon. It would connect

with the Central Pacific Railroad at Reno. They employed Nevada's Surveyor General, A.J. Hatch, to survey the line. John Davis later resigned as president of
the company and A.J. Hatch assumed the position.

A contract was signed in December 1880 for the construction of the first 31-mile section from Reno. Cold
and stormy weather delayed grading work; it was May
28, 1881, when the first spike was driven.

While anticipation of railroad service remained
high, life in Long Valley continued as usual. Maggie's
neighbor, Mrs. Chamberlin, gave birth to a baby daughter in July. Maggie, as before assisted her until she was
able to resume her household chores. Mary Louisa
Clark, now fourteen, was quite helpful around the
house. She took over at home while Maggie helped her
neighbors.

In August, Mary Louisa accompanied her stepfa-
ther, George Greeno on a business trip to Reno. It was
her first visit to that town, and her first to view a railroad train. They observed the N&O's construction
work in progress, and the Central Pacific train during
its stopover at Reno.

Convinced by Maggie that more winter feeding was
necessary to eliminate the loss of young calves and to
fatten the beef cattle for the early spring market,
George Greeno purchased 158 acres of land from Henry
Bereman in March 1882. That was the first of several
tracts they were to acquire in the years ahead. The land
was in Byrd Flat, four miles north of the Greeno home
ranch. It gave them meadowland needed to increase
their hay production and additional winter pasture.

George and Charlie Clark had been able to handle
most of the ranch work, except on cattle drives when
they hired extra vaqueros. With the additional land
more help was required during the harvest and winter
feeding. They hired a twenty-three year old ranch boy

named Arthur Franklin DeWitt, who had been raised in Honey Lake Valley, to assist with the heavier work, George, now sixty-six years old, was beginning to find some of the ranch work burdensome, especially the long hard days in the saddle during the rodeos and long cattle drives.

Maggie, in the prime of life at forty-four years, had mastered all the aspects of the livestock operation. She

Maggie Greeno in her prime (c. 1880s). Photo from Philbrook family album.

had indoctrinated Charlie Clark with most of the knowledge she had accumulated over the years, and was teaching ten-year-old "G" Greeno the rudiments of the business.

George had provided his son, who all members of the family were calling "G", with a gentle saddle horse, and was letting him ride along on the rodeos and drives to learn the tricks used in the cattle business.

It was September of 1882 before the N&O rails were laid to the Dave Evans ranch in the upper end of Long Valley, 31 miles from Reno. That station was named Oneida, and trains started carrying passengers and freight over the line on October 2, 1882. Meylert's Reno-Susanville stage started connecting with the N&O Railroad at Oneida, where the passengers boarded the train to Reno. If Meylert's stage was late the N&O would wait for it, sometimes several hours.

Not many stockmen used the N&O Railroad for shipping livestock. It meant extra work and confusion for both the cattle and men. Loading at Oneida on the narrow gauge stock cars, then unloading and reloading at Reno on the standard gauge Central Pacific. They found it faster and easier on the stock to drive them overland by the most direct route to Reno for loading.

In October 1883, Rueben Chamberlin announced that he had sold his property to F.D. Bennett from Sierra Valley. George and Maggie were surprised he had not mentioned he wished to sell. They would have again considered buying the ranch, in, order to get the meadowland along the creek. Maggie told Mrs. Chamberlin to let them know if their deal did not work out, because George would be interested in buying the property.

Maggie had begun to notice that her sixteen-year-old daughter Mary Louisa, was paying a lot of attention to their ranch hand Arthur F. DeWitt. She was spending a lot of time engaging him in conversation, and often

Wedding picture of Maggie's daughter, Mary Louisa Clark, and Arthur F. DeWitt (1883). Photo from Philbrook family album.

sought his help in catching and saddling her horse. She rode with him and her brother Charlie when they were moving cattle. It was also obvious to Maggie that Arthur was smitten with Mary Louisa.

The latter part of October 1883, Robert Ross, an early settler in the valley, completed a deal with Frank M. Rowland of Sierra Valley for the sale of his ranch. The Ross family announced they were moving to Reno to reside. The residents of Long Valley were sorry to have their longtime neighbors leave. Maggie and some of the neighbor ladies arranged for a party at the Ross home to wish them farewell.

Shortly after the party, Maggie and her family made plans for the wedding of her daughter, Mary Louisa, and Arthur Franklin DeWitt. Mary was seventeen and he was twenty-five. His mother, Mrs. George Fry, was a longtime Honey Lake Valley resident.

The gala affair took place at the Greeno home in February 1884. The young couple were united in marriage by the Reverend Mr. Spoon. The ceremony was performed in the presence of relatives and friends. After a short honeymoon in Reno, they returned to the Greeno ranch to reside.

With the additional hay land, the Greenos began to increase their herd. At each rodeo they would purchase young heifers from the other stockmen. The three young men—Arthur DeWitt and Maggie's two sons Charlie and G—did all the branding of the newly purchased livestock as well as the Greeno calves.

In June 1884, Albert E. Ross, whose ranch in Long Valley was a few miles south of the one newly purchased by Frank Rowland, began the construction of a fine new residence: a sixteen-room mansion which when finished, was the most elaborate of any home in Lassen County. It became known as the "White House" and over the years became the site of many Long Valley social events.

Jennie Chapman, Maggie's daughter, gave birth to a

baby boy they named John on June 7,1884. News of the birth reminded Maggie of her own son Alonzo, whom she had not seen since she left him with the Philbrooks when she and Charles Clark first moved to Susanville. He would now be twenty-four years old. She renewed her efforts to find him, a campaign of letter writing to every county sheriff in California brought no results.

The N&O Railroad continued to be a disappointment to the valley ranchers. It was revitalized in October 1884, and started laying track to the junction House. The project was completed in December, and the terminal was moved to that point. In four years, the construction had progressed only thirty-seven miles.

The company changed its name to Nevada and California Railroad Company in 1885. Regular service began from Reno to the Junction House where freight and stage lines then met the train.

There was very little precipitation during the winter of 1884-1885, and the wild grass did not grow very high. Settlers in the upper end of Long Valley built a dam and called it the Long Valley Reservoir. Ranchers in the lower part of the valley were highly incensed. In the first part of May, a charge of giant powder destroyed the dam. No one was surprised, and no one claimed to know who planted the charge.

The dry weather caused the vegetation to become exceedingly dry by mid-summer. On the morning of August 13, a fire started in the sage brush southwest of the Greeno's ranch. The wind was blowing away from Greeno's toward the Willow Ranch. When it was determined their property was not in the line of fire, Maggie instructed Charlie Clark, G Greeno and Arthur DeWitt to grab shovels, mount their horses and go help the Steinbergers. When they arrived, they found other neighboring hands had also arrived to fight the fire. Flames fed by the fire's wind leaped 20 feet in the air.

Several hours later, the volunteers succeeded in saving the ranch house, out-buildings, and most of the crops. All fences were destroyed. One of the volunteers barely escaped being engulfed by fire, and was chased for 200 yards before he outran it. Mr. Steinberger was truly grateful to all the ranchers for saving his ranch. It was a totally exhausted group of men who dragged themselves back to the Greeno ranch where Maggie and Mary Louisa had dinner waiting for them.

Young cattlemen on a rodeo can usually find excitement that might not be in line with their roundup duties. That happened on the September rodeo. Charlie Clark and Arthur DeWitt from the Greeno ranch, Lem Lemmon from the Lemmon ranch, and James Miller Jr. from the Miller ranch were involved in one such instance, written up as follows in the *Sierra Valley Leader* on September 25, 1885.

On the 7th of September a large California Lion weighing about 175 pounds., was killed on Fort Sage Mountain on the eastside of Long Valley. The young heroes were Charlie Clark, Arthur DeWitt, James Miller Jr., and Lem Lemmon, these young vaqueros were on the rodeo, and being without arms met this foe each with his turn with the lasso. Not being successful with the lariats the beast escaped to a ledge a few yards distant and disappeared in sort of a cave. The boys bringing up the rear hurriedly dismounted. While two guarded the mouth of the cave, the other two bravely entered wearing a Dutchman like expression on their faces. Silence reigned supreme for a few minutes. When Lo! upon the morning air came a terrific roar and a crash of rocks, followed by a chorus of voices crying "Lookout boys there he goes".

"Don't let him pass", etc. and out rush boys and lion in hot pursuit, head and tail erect, eyes flashing fire and teeth gnashing. There was mounting in haste and seizing their lariats they made another attempt at lassoing him, but in vain, so they commenced a game of hide and seek with him among the boulders. Flinging rock upon rock at him. At last a 100 pound boulder took him behind the ear and he fell over, a vanquished foe. Our young heroes gave three cheers, and proceeded on their way, each bearing a trophy of this lately won battle.

(The above article was reprinted in the October 1, 1885 issue of the *Lassen Advocate*.)

Maggie was furious with Charlie and Arthur when she heard their story. She reprimanded them severely for endangering themselves and their horses in attacking such a dangerous animal without the benefit of weapons.

The drought finally broke in January 1886, when long Valley experienced one of its heaviest storms. Over 36 inches of snow fell in a period of two days, and then the weather warmed and rain melted all the snow. Long Valley Creek overflowed its banks along the entire length of the valley. The N&C Railroad suffered a number of washouts along its right-of-way, which brought train service to a halt. The wagon road bridge over Long Valley Creek was washed away by the high water. As the water rose Charlie, Arthur and G were kept busy herding the young cows and calves out of the low-lying meadow to corrals and open range on higher ground.

George Greeno was held in high esteem by his fellow cattlemen for his many years in the business. His financial success over the past eight years was attributed to his wife Maggie, and her twenty-three-year-old

George W. Greeno (c. 1880s). Photo from Clark family album.


son, Charlie Clark. They had made most of the business
decisions with his approval.

When he reached seventy years of age in April 1886,

Maggie, the boys and his twelve-year old daughter Anna Frances arranged a surprise birthday party for him. Neighboring cattlemen and their families were invited to stop by and enjoy a glass of Champagne, and Anna Frances served each a slice of Maggie's delicious cake.

That same year on April 14, Mary Louisa and Arthur DeWitt became the proud parents of a baby boy. He was named Charles Arthur after her brother, Charlie Clark, and her husband, Arthur. Maggie was on hand to help Mary Louisa.

Winter snows the following year were accompanied by a strong wind throughout the valley. Drifting snow covered much of the feed on the open range, the cattlemen with hay in stacks started early in March to round up their cattle and bring them into their corrals to feed. They were also able to retire their sleighs, which had been required for transportation during most of the winter.

Hay was in short supply and the ranches that had any to spare were offered top prices for their surplus. Some Long Valley ranchers moved their cattle to the Reno feed yards, where hay was shipped in on the Central Pacific Railroad from the Sacramento Valley. The Greeno ranch managed to squeeze by with sufficient hay to feed their herd, but with no surplus to sell. However, they had a good herd of well-fed, prime steers to sell later in the year, when the price of beef returned to normal.

In March the operator of the stage station on the Bennett ranch (formerly Chamberlin station) decided to no longer serve the stage. Charles Sherman, the stage operator, prevailed upon Maggie and George to accommodate the passengers until he could arrange for another stopping place. The April 7, 1887, edition of the *Lassen Advocate* carried the following notice.

The Bennett place in Long Valley, kept by F. Nash until recently is now closed, and all the stage passengers are accommodated for the present at Geo. Greeno's. Mr. Greeno does not wish to keep a public station and is doing so now only as a matter of accommodation until other arrangements can be perfected. Uncle Geo., and his estimable wife know just how to entertain the public, and many who travel this road often, regret that they cannot be induced to keep public house.

On April 26, 1887, Maggie and her family made a train trip to Reno to attend the April 28 wedding of her son Thomas A. Oakes to Miss Abbie E. Nash. The ceremony was performed by Rev. C.L. Fisher of Reno. This was the first time that most of the family had the opportunity to ride the train from the Junction House to Reno.

Shortly after returning from the wedding, Mary Louisa and Arthur DeWitt broke the news to Maggie and the family that they were going to accept a position on a cattle ranch in Nevada, and would be leaving Long Valley. Maggie tried to discourage their moving, arguing that Mary Louisa had not been in the best of health since the birth of her baby, and should remain where medical attention could be obtained without a great amount of delay. Maggie's pleas fell on deaf ears. In May the DeWitts left the Greeno ranch and moved to Nevada.

After Arthur DeWitt left the ranch, Maggie contacted her brother Bill West, who was an employee of J.D. Byers, on his ranch in Honey Lake Valley. Maggie tried to persuade Bill to come and work on the Greeno ranch but Bill declined the offer, indicating that he would rather not work for relatives.

Maggie's son-in-law Francis Chapman stopped by the ranch on his way from Alturas. He was enroute south to look into the possibility of moving to that area. Maggie discussed the unsuccessful attempts she had in trying to locate the Philbrooks and her long-lost son Alonzo Kelly. Francis suggested that she write to every county clerk in California and ask if there were any Alonzo Philbrooks or Alonzo Kellys registered to vote in their county, and if so what their addresses were. Maggie took his suggestion and undertook the task of writing to every county clerk.

In June the Chapmans moved to Reno, and Jennie and her children stopped to visit at the Greeno ranch. Jennie was surprised to see her uncle Bill West, who was also visiting Maggie. Many years had passed since she had last seen her uncle and they had a lot of reminiscing and catching up to do. Maggie was delighted to see her grandchildren. She had never seen her grandson who had been born in Modoc County.

While Jennie was there, Maggie decided to have a family reunion. She sent for her new daughter-in-law, Abbie, and her husband Tom, who with the financial help of the Greenos, had established his own cabinet shop in Susanville.

The first week of August, seventy-one-year-old George Greeno and Charlie Clark drove a herd of 52 beef cattle to the Virginia City market. On their return trip, they noticed work was proceeding on the railroad grade through the Ross ranch. They stopped and asked if Ross had decided not to take the legal action he had threatened against the N&O Railroad. The foreman informed them the railroad company had decided to go ahead with the project, and fight the right-of-way dispute out in court later.

An annual tradition developed in Long Valley for the Albert E. Ross family. When their children returned for the holidays from their studies at the normal school in San Jose, they held an open house at the "White House", their fine new mansion. All the residents of Long Valley were invited to attend and participate in the activities. The Greeno family attended, enjoying the opportunity to meet and socialize with their neighbors and friends.

The past few years George Greeno had been moving his herd from the desert to the meadows over the mountains in Last Chance Country, in Plumas County. It was a strenuous operation rounding up the scattered herd over miles of desert and Fort Sage Mountain, cutting out the prime beef for market, and branding the young calves before driving them to summer pastures By the spring of 1888, seventeen-year-old G Greeno had become a great help to his father and half-brother, Charlie, and also a great pride to Maggie.

In 1888 the railroad again reorganized under the name of Nevada California and Oregon Railroad Company. By May, the tracks had reached the Doyle Ranch in Long Valley 57.75 miles from Reno. Endeavoring to stimulate revenue, the company started running special excursions over the line from Reno. On June 6, a special picnic excursion was run from Reno to Red Rock, a distance of 48 miles. It was such a success the company continued the excursions each weekend during the summer months.

The railroad terminal at Doyle was helpful to the Long Valley residents. They could take the train at Doyle and ride directly to Reno. The Susanville stage and freight wagons shortened their runs by meeting the train at Doyle. By September the railroad had extended its rails into Honey Lake Valley. Its terminal was then established at Leigan, a point near the southeastern tip of Honey Lake.

Maggie reached her half century mark on June 3,

1888. Although she did not rejoice at turning fifty, she enjoyed the afternoon tea with the Long Valley ladies who helped her observe the occasion.

On New Years Day 1889, a most unusual event took place in Long Valley: a total eclipse of the sun. Most of the residents watched it through smoke covered glass. The NC&O ran a special excursion from Reno to Leigan for the Nevada passengers to view the eclipse.

A big snow storm settled over the area later in January, and the Greeno ranch struggled to get feed to their stranded herds on the desert.

In the spring, Maggie received a letter from her daughter Mary Louisa DeWitt. She indicated that she was not feeling well and was having difficulty getting her breath. Maggie became fearful that Mary Louisa was not getting proper care, and that her two-year-old son Charles was also not getting proper attention.

Maggie had Charlie Clark harness their best team and hitch them to the surrey. The two of them made the day-long trip to the ranch in Nevada near Pyramid Lake. On their arrival they found Mary Louisa in bed. She had hardly been able to get around and care for young Charles Arthur.

After a day of resting and taking care of her daughter and little Charles, Maggie told Arthur that she and Charlie were going to take Mary and the boy back to Long Valley, where she could care for them and get the medical assistance Mary needed. In no uncertain terms, she expressed her displeasure with Arthur for bringing Mary Louisa so far away from help and medical aid.

Early the next day, Charlie Clark loaded Mary Louisa and the boy into the surrey with Maggie, then started the long drive back across the desert. They arrived at the Greeno ranch at dusk.

The following day, Maggie sent word by the stage driver to the doctor in Susanville, requesting he come to

Long Valley and treat Mary Louisa. Two days later the doctor arrived by horse and buggy. After his examination he concluded that she had contracted consumption. Maggie was instructed to keep her isolated from the rest of the family in a well-ventilated room with lots of fresh air. He ordered Mary to stay in bed and rest. The doctor left medicine to relieve her congestion and some tonic to stimulate her appetite. He told Maggie to feed her as much as she would eat to build up her strength.

Maggie spent the next two months in a desperate attempt to nurse Mary Louisa back to health. Fifteen-year-old Anna Frances was pressed into service, taking care of young Charles Arthur's many needs. The doctor stopped by on his occasional trips to Byrd Flat or Long Valley to check on Mary Louisa.

In June it became apparent that her condition had deteriorated, and she was not going to recover. Maggie sent word to Arthur DeWitt to come to her bedside. On June 24,1889, Mary Louisa died and her body was laid to rest in the small cemetery at Willow Ranch in Long Valley.

Both Maggie and Charlie Clark felt that if she had received the proper medical attention when she first began to feel ill she might have recovered. They were quite frank in expressing their opinions to Arthur, who himself was deeply grieved by the loss of his beloved wife.

Knowing that he was in no position to care for his son by himself, Arthur made no objection when Maggie told him she would keep the boy and raise him in a family environment. It was quite an undertaking for Maggie at fifty-one years to take on the responsibility of raising a two-year-old boy. She had the help of Anna Frances in looking after him. His Uncle Charlie and

Arthur F. DeWitt and son Charles "Cap" DeWitt (c. 1885). Photo from Philbrook family album.

Uncle G entertained the lad when their ranch chores permitted.

Early in the fall, after the men had finished putting up the hay for winter feed, they went to the mountains and rounded up 189 head of prime steers they had sold to H.F. Daughtery of Douglas County, Nevada. Charlie and G drove the herd to the Reno stockyards for Mr. Daughtery.

While at Reno they attended the Nevada State Fair, and on their way home they stopped at the Willow Ranch to look over the fine new house J.M. Steinberger was having built. They purchased a sack of the prizewinning Steinberger apples grown in the ranch orchard.

In the fall of 1889, the Reverend Mr. Clark began to hold church services in the Long Valley schoolhouse every other Sunday. This was the first time church services were held in Long Valley. Maggie insisted on her entire family attending, as did most other residents in the lower end of Long Valley.

All hands from the Greeno ranch were actively involved in the fall rodeo in the Plumas mountains. After separating the stock for market and branding the new calves, the herd was driven to the ranch. The young cows and calves they held on the ranch to feed. The prime beef cattle they now loaded on the NC&O at Doyle for shipment to the Reno stockyards. The remainder of the herd was turned out to graze on the desert.

# CHAPTER XV

## LAKE GREENO

The heaviest rainstorm that had ever been known to fall in Long Valley came in December 1889. All the creeks overflowed their banks. The rain changed to snow during the first week in January, leaving eight to ten inches of heavy snow on the ground. All the men at the Greeno ranch were kept busy hauling hay to feed the cows and calves.

A scarcity of hay in the valley brought the price to $20 a ton. Some stockmen were compelled to ship in hay from the Sacramento Valley. Others in desperation drove many poor cattle to Reno to have them fed in the feed lots.

Anna Frances, who had not been feeling well, took the NC&O train to Reno, where she was to receive medical attention. She was accompanied by Charlie Clark who, after seeing her settled with the Chapman family, took the Central Pacific train to San Francisco on January 30, 1890, where he enrolled in the Healds Business College.

Meanwhile, Maggie's inquires to the county clerks was beginning to give her some hope of locating her long-lost son. She had learned from the county clerk of Santa Clara county that there was a farmer named Alonzo Philbrook registered in the San Jose area, with a post office address at Alviso, California. Maggie at once wrote a letter to him, explaining who she was and asking if he was the Alonzo Philbrook that was at the

Chaparral House in Butte County in the 1860s. If so what information could he give her about her son?

About three months later, she received a letter from an attorney in San Jose stating that he was writing on behalf of Mr. Philbrook, who was now sixty years old and not in the best of health. Mr. Philbrook was sorry that they had not searched her out many years earlier, but they had become so attached to her son that when they decided to leave Butte county, and she had not come for him, they took him along with them to Santa Clara county. They had raised him as their own son, even to giving him the name of Philbrook. He had been educated in the public school, and at present was apprenticing as a saddle maker with the firm of Main and Winchester in San Francisco.

When Maggie received the letter she was again tied down with the care of three-year-old Charles Arthur DeWitt, and with Anna Frances who was in poor health. Unable to go to San Francisco to meet with Alonzo in person, she wrote him a letter in care of Main and Winchester. She explained in detail who she was and how they became separated, and of her long search to locate him. Maggie also wrote to Charlie Clark, who was attending business school in San Francisco, and asked him to contact Alonzo and get acquainted with him, and to answer any questions he might have about the family.

Water from the winter storms kept the creeks high well into March. When the spring rodeo, delayed by the high water, was finally held, the stockmen were pleased to find their cattle on the desert were in much better shape than they had expected. As soon as the rodeo was over, the ranchers were busy plowing and sowing their crops. With Charlie away at business school, the Greeno ranch was operating shorthanded. Seventy-four-year-old George Greeno, who everyone in the valley now called "Uncle George," tried hard to help out. Most of the heavier work fell to his eighteen-year-old son G Greeno. They still had to hired a couple of extra hands during the rodeo and planting season.

Work started again in July 1890, to extend the NC&O line from Leigan to Brubeck's place at Lower Hot Springs in Honey Lake Valley. The last rail on that extension was laid in October, and that terminal was named Amedee, 79 miles from Reno.

Anna Frances' health seemed somewhat improved in November, and she was able to care for little Charles DeWitt. Maggie boarded the train at Doyle and went to San Francisco, where she was reunited with her thirty-year-old son Alonzo Kelly, now known as Philbrook, it was a very emotional experience for her. It wasn't quite as intense for Alonzo, as he had learned to consider the Philbrooks to be his family. However, he was glad to know his natural mother, and to learn that he had half-brothers and sisters and several half-nieces and nephews.

Maggie was amazed at the many changes that had taken place in San Francisco since she had last been in the city. It was now a booming, bustling seaport city, much like she remembered Boston to be—except now, steam-powered ferries and ocean-going vessels plied the bay. Only a few high-masted schooners were visible. Horse-pulled streetcars were numerous. The stores were filled with exotic merchandise from all over the world. Millinery stores and dress shops displayed hats and readymade dresses and gowns she never knew existed. The opportunity to attend live theater with her newly found son was a most pleasant experience. She spent several days getting acquainted with Alonzo, and enjoying the big city sights. When Maggie returned to Long Valley, she brought a couple of new hats and dresses, and presents for all the family. She even brought home a live canary in a brass cage. She had found the bird in a pet shop, and was so taken with its cheerful song that she could not resist the desire to have it in her home.

George Greeno listened with great interest as Maggie explained the new steam-powered ships she had seen, and the luxurious steam ferry boats that crossed the Bay. it was hard for the old seaman to believe that so many changes in ships had taken place in the past forty years since he had given up the sea.

Maggie and George drove their surrey to Susanville in December, stopping along the way to visit friends. They spent several days with Tom and Abbie Oakes. Maggie told Tom all about her trip to San Francisco and her meeting with his half-brother Alonzo.

Over a few years. the Honey Lake land and Water Company had acquired a vast acreage of the desert land east of Honey Lake. The Company wanted to subdivide the land and sell it to settlers. In order to provide the required irrigation water, the company explored the idea of building a reservoir on Long Valley Creek, with a dam in the narrows where the creek exited Long Valley and entered Honey Lake Valley.

On January 8, 1891, L.H. Taylor, the project engineer, filed a notice claiming the dam site and the area covered by the reservoir. That survey disclosed the high water in the reservoir would cover most of the meadowland on the old Chamberlin Station Ranch, which was then owned by the estate of R.S. Bennett, and the adjacent ranch to the south. It would also back the water up to within a few hundred yards of the Greeno ranch.

By this time Maggie had assumed most of the decision-making authority for the Greeno ranch business. George's age and his rheumatism had begun to take its toll on the old sailor's vigor and enthusiasm, Maggie was still a young, spirited fifty-two year old. She was

Maggie's three sons (c. 1890s). Left to right Charlie Clark, G
Greeno, Thomas Oakes. Photo from Philbrook family album.

anxious to continue building the cattle business for her
sons Charlie and G.

Maggie invited Tom and Abbie Oakes to the ranch on February 12, 1891, for Tom's thirty-fifth birthday. She prepared a special dinner for the occasion. During the festivities, when George was out of earshot, the family discussed plans to hold a surprise reception for him in April on his seventy-fifth birthday.

The latter part of March, they completed plans for George's birthday festivities. All Long Valley ranchers and their families were invited. On Sunday, April 12, friends began to drop in from far and wide to wish George a happy birthday. The party and the huge birthday cake baked by Maggie and served by Anna Frances took him completely by surprise. Alonzo Philbrook sent a letter from San Francisco wishing him many more years of health and happiness. In the letter, he disclosed that he and Miss Susan Martin, a native of Santa Cruz, had been married, and they planned to continue living in San Francisco.

The Honey Lake Land and Water Company started work clearing the dam site of sagebrush. They hired all the teams and drivers they could roundup. The company also began negotiations to purchase all the private land that would be under the reservoir site. As the number of workmen on the dam increased, the Company built a construction camp between the dam site and Leigan Station. They called it Camp Taylor. The Company also decided to name the reservoir Lake Greeno, in honor of George Greeno, the first settler in that part of Long Valley, and an adjacent prominent land owner.

Maggie Greeno had for many years been eyeing the Chamberlin Station as ideal for their ranch expansion because of its close proximity to their home ranch, and for its fine meadowland. They had never been able to reach an agreement with the various owners to acquire the property. With meadow now about to be flooded by the proposed reservoir, Maggie decided they should look elsewhere for additional meadowland.

It had been Maggie's intention to find a hundred acres of meadowland relatively close to their ranch. When word got around the Greeno's were looking for land, they were approached by Jonathan C. Roberts who had accumulated vast land and livestock holdings in the upper end of Long Valley. His health was beginning to fail, and he offered to sell all his land and livestock, as he wished to retire. His property consisted of over one thousand acres of land and several hundred head of livestock.

When the Greeno's were confronted with that offer, George at first dismissed it as being far too large and expensive for them to undertaken After a few days of thinking about it and talking it over among themselves, Maggie, Charlie and G came to the conclusion it would be a great challenge, and would vastly expand their livestock operation. Maggie cautioned that it would be wise to explore all the possibilities, good and bad, of the deal. She persuaded George that they should take a closer look at the properties, to determine exactly what type of a deal could be made with Roberts.

Maggie and George took their buggy, and Charlie and G accompanied them on horseback. All four rode the 25 miles south to the Roberts ranch. They went into details with Mr. Roberts to determine what type of financial arrangements he was willing to accept. Jonathan Roberts told them that because the Greenos had such a fine reputation as livestock operators, and for their honest dealings, he would be willing to take a mortgage on the property that could be paid off over ten years, if they could purchase the livestock for cash.

Maggie and her boys decided to take a closer look at the property. Roberts escorted the four of them around the main ranch and showed them the livestock that was on the ranch at that time. The Greenos stayed another day looking over the ranch and discussing the deal. Maggie and George drove their buggy back home, while Charlie and G spent another two days riding to the Roberts outlying properties and looking over his livestock on the open range.

After returning home, the four family members spent the next several evenings discussing the proposed deal. Charlie Clark, just a few months out of business school, explained what he had learned about the use of leverage and credit. His idea was that if Roberts would sell off the prime beef he had on the open range, the Greenos had sufficient cash on hand to pay for the balance of the Roberts herd. The young stock would be coming prime the next spring, and from then on should more than make the mortgage payments.

Old "Uncle George," who had always dealt in cash, was skeptical that it would work out as Charlie had calculated. He pointed out additional help would be needed because of the long distance from their home ranch. Charlie countered by showing him how much additional profit the livestock sales should show at the end of each year as they reduced the interest on the mortgage.

Maggie and G sided with Charlie, and George finally agreed to present their offer to Roberts, after admonishing the boys that it would be their obligation to work off the mortgage; that he was not going to mortgage his ranch for them under any condition.

Jonathan Roberts readily accepted the Greeno offer. On June 29, 1891, he and his wife deeded the Greenos and Charlie Clark their main ranch property of 480 acres, and accepted the mortgage. After making some adjustments in the price of the livestock to compensate for some of the older cows that Roberts had sold in the meantime, the Roberts deeded the balance of the outlying property, some 500 acres, to George and Charlie. The Roberts moved to Reno shortly thereafter.

The Greeno ranch properties were now scattered from Byrd Flat in Honey Lake Valley to the newly acquired land in the upper end of Long Valley. Greeno and Clark converted their new ranch into a base camp, and employed a herdsman and his wife to reside at the camp and ride herd on the cattle grazing in that area. All hands from both ranches assisted in the rodeos, and in harvesting the hay on both ranches for winter feeding.

The winter social activities in Long Valley commenced with a dance. On a Friday in early November the young people of Long Valley tended to the employees of the Honey Lake Land and Water Company a social. Their plan was to surprise the people at Camp Taylor. The Surprisers furnished the instrumental and vocal music, and served a lunch at 12 o'clock. After which dancing was resumed until 4 A.M. Maggie, Charlie Clark and G Greeno were among those that enjoyed the first of a series of dances held in the camp boarding house and in Long Valley that winter.

A few days after that gala event, Maggie took her daughter Anna Frances to San Francisco. They visited Maggie's son Alonzo and his wife Susan. Maggie and Susan enjoyed showing Anna Frances the sights. Together they shopped, went to see live theater, and rode the street cars. After a week in the city they returned to Long Valley with a supply of new clothes for Anna Frances and another canary.

The 1891 holiday season was a festive occasion for Maggie and her family. Tom and Abbie Oakes spent Christmas at the ranch, along with Charlie Clark, G Greeno, Anna Frances, and Maggie's five-year-old grandson Charles Arthur DeWitt. He provided the childish enthusiasm for Christmas. Maggie's brother,

Bill West rode his horse from Janesville to have Christmas dinner with them.

Spring came early in 1892: the February weather was pleasant, allowing work on the Lake Greeno Dam

to get underway in earnest. Honey Lake Land and Water Company had a great number of teamsters at work moving earth into the base of the dam.

The Greeno ranch that year started holding rodeos in two areas. After the stock was rounded up and the calves branded on the desert and Fort Sage Mountain, they turned their attention to the upper regions of Long Valley, and started the roundup of cattle on the former Roberts range. After branding there they drove them to the mountain pasture in Plumas County.

Maggie's youngest daughter, Anna Frances Greeno (c. 1890s). Photo from Philbrook family album.

Long Valley residents watched with interest the progress being made on the dam that would ultimately flood the meadows along the creek. Many of the ranchers who could spare the time took jobs with their teams and scrapers. Others sold hay and grain to feed the horses and mules working on the project. Interest in the construction became widespread. The following article appeared in the March 31, edition of the Reno *Gazette*.

## LONG VALLEY RESERVOIR
H. Peterson and Walter Smith who are interested in the Long Valley Land and Water

Company's work called at the Gazette office this morning. These gentlemen were attracted to Long Valley, seeing an ad in the paper about a year ago. Dissatisfied with their homes in California moved over the mountains at once, and purchased a home, and went to work on the reservoir. The Company has 42 teams and scrapers working on the structure.

They expect to make a home on the arid plains of Honey Lake, that will be a credit to anybody or any country. They expect the dam will be ready to catch the floods of next winter and then they will commence seeding the land.

Many of the settlers who have gone there to settle are already building homes on this plain. There are about 90 men at work on the reservoir.

Team and scraper used on Lake Greeno Dam construction, Long Valley, Lassen County, California (1892). Photo courtesy Lassen Historical Society, Susanville, California.

Construction crew on Lake Greeno Dam. Long Valley, Lassen County, California (1892). Photo courtesty Lassen Historical Society, Susanville, California.

The number of people working on the dam and living at Camp Taylor continued to increase, and settlers began to move to the desert and build homes. In March 1892, the U.S. Postal Service established a post office at Camp Taylor under the name of Lake Greeno, California. People living in the area then started receiving their mail at the Lake Greeno post office.

Bill West, Maggie's brother, stopped by the Greeno ranch to visit in August. He informed Maggie that he planned to marry a widow, Mrs. Eliza L. Ramsey. Her husband had been deceased for some time, leaving her with six children. Two girls were grown and no longer at home, and the other four were teenagers. Maggie told Bill that at forty-nine years of age, she thought it was time for him to settle down. Everyone at the Greeno ranch wished him a happy marriage.

William H. West and Mrs. Eliza L. Ramsey were united in marriage at Janesville on September 1, 1892.

Present were her six children, Maggie and George Greeno and Charlie Clark.

By September, work on the dam at Lake Greeno was well along. The NC&O Railroad ran a special excursion from Reno to Leigan, for the Nevada people to observe the work in progress. Company representatives met the train at Leigan, and conveyed the people that came in covered carriages drawn by good horses to Camp Taylor. They viewed the work on the dam, which when completed was designed to be 115 feet high, 500 feet wide at the base, and 1,000 feet from bank to bank. It was expected to back up water for six miles and cover 1,281 acres to an average depth of 14 feet. Seventy men and 50 teams were at work. Outlet gates of solid masonry were being built at the side of the dam.

G Greeno celebrated his twentieth birthday on September 23, by going to Susanville with his father, mother and sister to attend the opening of the annual District Fair. They stayed with Tom and Abbie Oakes and visited with friends. On their return to the ranch, Charlie Clark went to the fair for its closing days.

Shortly thereafter the men started the fall rodeo in the Plumas mountains. They moved the cattle both ways, those farthest north to the home ranch, those found farther south to the Roberts, or south ranch. After separating out the prime beef, they put the cows, calves and young stock in pasture on both ranches for winter feeding. The other stock was turned out to range on Fort Sage Mountain, as the desert was now taken up by settlers waiting irrigation water from Lake Greeno.

They drove a small herd of prime beef to the Virginia City market. On their return they stopped in Reno and called on Jonathan Roberts to pay their first installment on the mortgage, using the funds they had received from the cattle sale.

After the men had returned to the ranch, Maggie

and Anna Frances made a sojourn by train to San Francisco to visit the Philbrooks. Maggie purchased another canary, to replace her first one that had died of old age.

On her return, Maggie noticed water in Long Valley Creek had begun to puddle up behind the dam. The construction crews were working feverishly to finish the structure, hoping to hold back the winter run-off. The outlet gates were finished and the overflow cut beside the dam to drain off any excess water was ready. All that remained was to complete raising the top of the structure a few more-feet to get it above-the bottom of the overflow cut. The chief engineer hired every available team and scraper he could find to move dirt, in an effort to complete the project before the winter storms filled the reservoir.

The forces of nature that had spent eons carving out the channel for the creek to discharge its water into Honey Lake were not to be outdone by the efforts of men. The early fall rains had already accumulated a considerable volume of water behind the uncompleted dam, and Lake Greeno had begun to fill, to the delight of the Company and the settlers.

The last days of November 1892, nature turned loose her fury with heavy rains throughout the Long Valley Creek drainage area and surrounding areas of Northern California. The water began to rise rapidly behind the unfinished dam.

The engineers opened the outlet gate to discharge as much water as possible from behind the unfinished dam. Torrential rains throughout the watershed of Long Valley Creek overflowed the creek's banks. Water reaching Lake Greeno soon rose above the top of the dam and overflowed the structure with such force that it soon breached the dam. By the following morning much of the earth, and all of the labor, planning, and money that had gone into the dam, as well as the water it was supposed to have restrained, had disappeared down nature's original channel into Honey Lake.

Lake Greeno had come into existence and disappeared in a matter of days. Talk of reviving the project persisted among the Company officials and the desert settlers for a few years. Finances were not forthcoming and the entire project died a natural death. The Lake Greeno Post Office continued to serve the people of the area, but Camp Taylor was abandoned. Over a period of time it was dismantled and carted away by settlers needing the lumber for buildings or firewood. The meadow along the creek returned to its original state.

The men on the Greeno ranches had their hands full looking after their large herds. The spring and fall rodeos, planting, hay harvests, cattle drives, loading cattle for market, and winter feeding kept them busy.

Maggie and Anna Frances were occupied looking after the well-being of Maggie's grandson, Charles DeWitt, and taking care of the many household chores. Maggie had to supervise Paiute Jack, the Indian who cultivated and irrigated the garden, fed the farm horses and dairy cow, and split the firewood, in addition to other various odd jobs around the ranch.

Charles DeWitt started school when he was six years old. Maggie, on one of her shopping trips to Milford, bought him a cap with a large bill, or sunshade. Unlike the wide brimmed hats the cattlemen wore, it soon attracted attention. Charles was quite fond of the cap, and in spite of its being too large, he wore it whenever he was outside. The ranch hands began to call him "Cap." The name was to stick with him throughout his life. Many people who called him Cap never knew his real name.

Anna Frances reached her nineteenth birthday, and G Greeno his twenty-first, in September 1893. Tom Oakes was doing quite well with the planing mill and shop: he had expanded his cabinet shop to include the manufacture of furniture.

Maggie wrote a letter to the San Francisco headquarters of the Honey Lake Land and Water Company, advising them the Greeno ranch would be interested in leasing the Chamberlin Station property. If they were planning to sell the property, she also wrote, the Greenos might consider purchasing it for the right price and terms.

The Company was badly in need of cash to pay the many debts it had accumulated during the final days of the dam construction. They agreed to give the Greeno ranch a lease on the property for a reasonable price if paid in advance.

The Greeno ranch took over the property with the expectation they could increase their hay production. Before the second year's lease was up, the water company determined that it would be impossible for them to refinance the dam project. They offered to sell the ranch to the Greenos, but they wanted cash.

Having used most of their surplus cash in the purchase of the Roberts' livestock, the Greenos were unable to come up with all the necessary cash, as George Greeno refused to mortgage his original holdings. After considerable dickering, Charlie Clark convinced the officials of the water company that they would be able to borrow against the mortgage that he and the Greenos were willing to execute for the property.

Early in 1895, the Greenos and the water company reached an agreement and the company sold them the property. The Greenos then moved into the old Chamberlin Station House. George was at first reluctant to move off the property he had resided on since first claiming it thirty-five years earlier. Maggie and the boys persuaded him that it was all right, because he could always move back if something went wrong with the deal. The big house was much more convenient and had a better barn and sheds for their equipment.

Charlie Clark at Chamberlin Station House, Long Valley (c. 1890s). Photo from Clark family album.

## CHAPTER XVI

# THE WILLOW RANCH

George Greeno turned eighty in April, 1896. Slowed by the infirmities of old age, he still endeavored to remain active to some degree in the ranch, although Maggie and her sons actually ran the business. Maggie prepared a small party for him, and invited all his friends to come and celebrate his birthday.

Charlie Clark, now thirty-two, became interested in attending the dances held at Milford, where he seemed to enjoy the company of the young ladies of that area. Whenever he made trips to Milford or Janesville, he found an excuse to stop at the McDermott ranch. It soon became obvious to the McDermotts and the Greenos that his interest in stopping had nothing to do with the ranch business, but was an excuse to ask Miss Emma McDermott to accompany him to some dance or social event.

Another development that was to eventually change things at the Greeno ranch occurred that year: Miss Catherine I. Robb, of Reno, came to Long Valley to teach school. Maggie, interested in seeing that her grandson Cap DeWitt had a good education, offered to let her board with them. Not many months had gone by before G Greeno was exchanging admiring glances with the attractive young teacher.

Meanwhile, Maggie's eldest son Tom Oakes expanded his furniture business in Susanville. Along with the manufacturing of furniture, he was also called upon to build caskets. To better serve that lucrative part of his business, Tom purchased the stock of T.H. Sanders' undertaking goods. He also purchased a hearse from H.N. Skadden, and was then able to provide all the services needed for a burial.

Maggie began to schedule her trips to Milford or Susanville on Saturdays, so that "Kate" Robb, the school teacher, could accompany her. They often stopped at the McDermott Ranch near Milford, where Maggie and Kate had the opportunity to get better acquainted with Emma McDermott, who had been attracting so much of Charlie's attention.

On November 11, 1896, Maggie and George were honored at a reception in their Long Valley home, commemorating their silver wedding anniversary. Friends and family members from Long Valley, Milford, Janesville and Susanville stopped by to pay their respects to the well-known and respected couple.

In the spring of 1897, Anna Frances, who had not been robust, began to require a great deal of medical attention. Both Maggie and Charlie Clark had taken her to doctors in Susanville and Reno. Her condition gradually deteriorated and she became completely bedridden by midsummer. On August 4, 1897, Anne Frances died quietly. The physician who was in attendance returned to Susanville and informed Tom Oakes his services were needed at the Greeno ranch. Her funeral was conducted by the Rev. Mr. Spoon at the Greeno residence on Friday, August 6th. Friends from Susanville, Janesville, Milford and the surrounding country were present.

The loss of Anna Frances was a very heart-wrenching experience for Maggie. Anna was the third daughter she had lost, and the second to the dreaded lung disease.

During late August many cattle buyers were in

Long Valley, seeking beef cattle for the market. Mr. Evans of Reno was buying cattle to be shipped to eastern buyers. He purchased 150 head from the Greeno ranch to be delivered to the stockyards in Nebraska. Charlie Clark and G Greeno agreed to accompany the cattle, to be sure they were properly loaded and unloaded for feeding and watering along the route. They loaded the cattle on the NC&O at Doyle station on September 2, 1897, and reloaded on the Central Pacific at Reno.

While Charlie and G were on their way to Nebraska with the cattle, Maggie and George were surprised to read an advertisement in the Reno Gazette by J.M. Steinberger offering-his Willow Ranch for sale. The advertisement outlined the extensive garden and orchard products grown on the ranch, the large acreage of wheat and hay, and the commodious farm house and large barns thereon. Included was all the ranch machinery and livestock.

When George drove the surrey to the NC&O station to pick up Charlie and G on their return from Nebraska, he stopped at the Willow Ranch and inquired of Jim Steinberger whether he had received any offers from his ad. Steinberger informed him that he had received a couple of inquiries, neither of which appeared to be a promising prospect. He then suggested that George consider buying Willow Ranch. Still in debt to Roberts and the Honey Lake Valley Land and Water Company, George dismissed the suggestion as being too expensive.

When George got home with the boys, he informed Maggie of the Steinberger proposal. Maggie and the boys began to discuss the merits of owning the Willow Ranch. They started to calculate how much the ranch was worth, how much it would add to their hay and barley production, and if it could be made to pay for itself.

George Greeno insisted they were wasting their time. Charlie and Maggie admitted he was probably right and did not push the issue, but they continued to turn the idea over in their minds as they went about their daily tasks.

During the fall rodeo, G's horse fell with him injuring his leg. At first it was feared the leg was broken, but it turned out to be a bad bruise. He was laid up for several days, and the leg remained sore for a couple of months, which caused him to limp as he walked.

Tom Oakes continued to expand his business. In the spring of 1898, he moved his shop into a building on Main Street below Union Street, and also began to sell marble and granite monuments. Maggie was quite proud of Tom's success, and the prompt manner in which he paid off the loan that the Greeno family had extended him.

Major changes continued to take place in Long Valley. During March Albert E. Ross, one of the earliest settlers in the valley, sold his ranch and dairy in Last Chance to Henry A. Butters of Oakland. Butters named the ranch Constantia, and did some remodeling on the "White House." He built a carriage house and a small chapel nearby.

The residents of the Milford area staged a Fourth of July celebration that year, and the Greenos used the occasion to visit with their friends. Charlie Clark confined most of his visiting to the McDermott family, and Miss Emma in particular. School being over for the summer, Miss Robb had returned to her parents home in Reno. G had to confine his interests to the ball game and races. The Spanish-American War had brought patriotism to a high pitch, and many stirring speeches were made during the day's activities.

A year had passed since Mr. Steinberger first offered the Willow Ranch for sale. He had hoped to find a buyer

such as Albert Ross had found in Henry Butters, one
that would pay him cash. No such buyer had came
forth, so at the Milford celebration, he approached
George Greeno requesting he make an offer on the Willow Ranch. On the way home George told Maggie and
the boys of Steinberger's request. They again began to
seriously discuss the pros and cons of taking on the Willow Ranch property and livestock, and the various ways
they might be able to finance such an undertaking. The
Roberts ranch holdings had worked out well: they still
had a couple of payments left on that mortgage. The
same was true of the Chamberlin ranch. The increase in
the number of livestock they had available to market
had been significant. They had accumulated a comfortable surplus of cash, which they now kept on deposit in
the newly formed Bank of Lassen County, in Susanville.
Although George would have felt more comfortable
with it buried in the backyard.

Maggie, George, Charlie and G met with Jim
Steinberger in order to determine how much income
the ranch produced from the hay and grain, and from
the many assorted vegetables, apples and other fruits.
After an extensive amount of figuring and discussion
among the four of them, they came to the conclusion
that Willow Ranch could provide enough additional hay
and grain to winter feed a great number of cattle. With
George reluctantly agreeing, they proposed to Jim
Steinberger that he give them an option to purchase the
ranch, for which they would give him a small cash payment. After the fall roundup when they sold their prime
beef, they would make a substantial payment, and give
him a note for the balance. The contract carried a stipu-
lation that the Greenos were to take possession of the
meadow and corrals for winter feeding, and that the
Steinbergers could remain in the house until spring.
Steinberger accepted their offer and gave them the op-

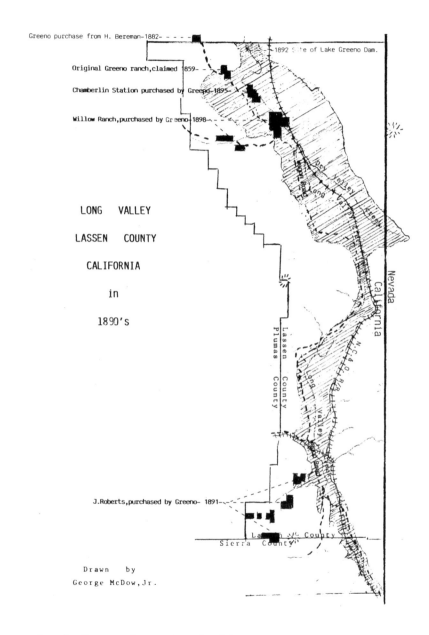

Greeno purchase from H. Bereman-1882- - - - -

Original Greeno ranch,claimed 1859- -

Chamberlin Station purchased by Greeno-1895-

Willow Ranch,purchased by Greeno-1898- -

1892 Site of Lake Greeno Dam.

LONG     VALLEY

LASSEN    COUNTY

CALIFORNIA

in

1890's

Nevada

California

Lassen County

Plumas County

Long Valley Creek

N.C.&.O. R.R.

J.Roberts,purchased by Greeno- 1891-

Lassen County

Sierra  County

Drawn    by
George McDow,Jr.

tion in September 1898. On November 3, the Greenos
made their initial payment and gave their note.

Steinberger then deeded the property to George Greeno and Charlie Clark.

Following the spring rodeo in 1899, the Steinbergers moved to Reno to live in retirement, and the Greeno family moved to Willow Ranch.

A big event for Charlie Clark took place an Sunday April 9, 1899. He and Emma McDermott were married at the home of her parents near Milford. The Rev. J.H. Rosen performed the ceremony in the presence of all members of the McDermott and Greeno families and several young friends of the bride and groom. The new-lywed couple moved to the Willow Ranch to live.

Not to be outdone by his older half-brother, G Greeno proposed to Miss Robb the young schoolmarm, whom he had been squiring to dances and social events. George "G" Greeno Jr. and Catherine Robb were married on August 30, 1899, in Reno. The young couple returned to the Willow Ranch after a short honeymoon.

Tom Oakes had become active in the fraternal order of I.O.O.F. in November 1899, he went to San Francisco, where he participated in the Golden Jubilee Parade of the Odd Fellows Lodge. While in San Francisco, Tom became acquainted with his half-brother Alonzo Philbrook, who then held an office in the San Francisco Odd Fellows Lodge.

Alonzo had been suffering from some bronchial problem which he thought had been brought on by the damp foggy climate of the bay area. Tom suggested that Alonzo consider moving to Lassen County's arid climate. Tom indicated to Alonzo that his furniture business was getting large and he could use the help of an experienced upholsterer. He suggested they might work out some type of an arrangement to combine their skills.

That November, the first complete general store in Long Valley was opened on the Constantia ranch by

R.A. Moncure. The people of the valley were delighted to have a store to supply their needs without having to make the long trip to Milford or Reno. To show their appreciation, on December 1 they gave Mr. Moncure what they thought was to be a surprise party. Moncure, having been tipped off about the coming event, surprised the party-goers by having prepared a sumptuous feast for the occasion. Many young couples, from the lower to the upper end of Long Valley, attended. Dancing commenced at 9 o'clock and continued until dawn. The excellent music consisted of two violins and a guitar.

Charlie and Emma Clark did not attend as Emma was heavy with child. Maggie accompanied G and his wife Kate. At sixty-one Maggie spent most of the evening visiting with others her age as they watched the young people dance the one-step and the turkey-trot.

An accident occurred near Willow Ranch on December 17, when Mrs. W.J. Robinson's horse was spooked while she was on her way to Buntingville. She was unable to control the frightened animal and the cart overturned, throwing her against a barbed wire fence and slashing her face and neck. Young Cap DeWitt, upon hearing the commotion, ran down the road and helped her to the Greeno house where Maggie applied first aid.

As soon as Mrs. Robinson regained her composure, Maggie had Cap harness her horse and hitch it to a buggy. After summoning Dr. Julian from Janesville, she drove Mrs. Robinson home and helped her into bed. When the doctor arrived, he administered treatment to her wounds and said she would soon recover, baring any internal injuries. Maggie stayed with her until her family made arrangements for her care.

Maggie made the first Christmas at Willow Ranch an extra festive occasion. Besides her husband George,

*240*

The Willows Ranch House, Maggie's home in Long Valley, Lassen
County, California, from 1899–1916 (house built in 1880s by J.M.
Steinberger). Photo courtesy Lassen Historical Society, Susanville,
California.

Storing hay in the barn at Willow Ranch, Doyle, California (1911).
Photo from Clark family album.

there were Charlie and Emma, G and Kate, and Cap DeWitt, all of whom lived at the ranch. She invited Tom and Abbie and folks from the neighboring ranches to drop by and enjoy a cup of eggnog, and partake in the joy of Christmas with them.

In her Christmas note to her son Alonzo and his wife Susan, Maggie mentioned that Tom had told her of Alonzo's health problem, and she suggested he consider

Maggie's son Alonzo Kelly Philbrook (c. 1890s). Photo from Philbrook family album.

Tom's proposal that he come to Lassen County to see if the dry climate would improve his condition.

The year ended on a happy note for Maggie and the family. On December 30, Emma Clark gave birth to their first child, a daughter they named Mary Estella.

In the spring of 1900, G Greeno had a new house constructed a few yards from the Willow Ranch house. He and his wife Kate, expecting their first child, moved into the new house in the early summer. Charlie Clark and his wife Emma continued to live in the Willow Ranch house with Maggie and George and young Cap DeWitt.

Alonzo Philbrook decided to take the advice of Maggie and his half-brother Tom Oakes and try the high altitude climate of Honey Lake Valley. He and his wife Susan moved to Susanville around the first of March 1900. Shortly after their arrival they purchased a lot on Nevada Street, and contracted to have a nice home built. Before the month was over, Alonzo Philbrook and Tom Oakes entered into a co-partnership in the furniture and undertaking business.

The spring rodeo that year was the first in which Maggie's grandson, fourteen-year-old Cap DeWitt, was allowed to participate. It was also the last in which George Greeno, then eighty-four, endeavored to take a part. He drove his horse and buggy to the round-up corral where he watched the branding, and looked over the beef cattle that Charlie and G were separating for the market. The excitement and exertion was almost too much for the old cattleman. On his return to Willow Ranch he was confined to his bed for several days. The doctor administered medicine to ease the pain In his aching joints, and advised him to rest as much as possible. In May he suffered a setback and it appeared that he might not recover. Maggie sent for Tom Oakes to come to the ranch, thinking that his undertaking services might be needed. However, the tough old cattleman regained his strength, and was soon out doing the ranch chores he was able to handle.

Shortly after Tom Oakes returned to Susanville, he experienced a painful injury: he lost two joints of his index finger while operating a rabbet saw in his shop.

A disastrous fire struck Susanville on the morning of June 6, 1900, burning forty buildings in three blocks on the south side of Main Street, between Roop and Union Streets. Fortunately, the shop and store of Oakes' and Philbrook's was on the north side of the street and escaped the conflagration.

Replacing the homes and buildings destroyed by the fire created business for the shop of Oakes and Philbrook. The shop was kept busy making doors, windows and cabinets in addition to furniture. This boom to their business prompted the two men to consider constructing a larger store building. They favored the lot on the corner of Main and Gay Street. Lacking sufficient funds, Tom Oakes once again turned to the Greeno Ranch for finances. This time, Charlie and Maggie asked Tom and Alonzo for a full financial statement, and an estimate on the cost of the lot and building.

Tom, somewhat exhausted from the loss of his finger and many years of hard work, decided in August to let Alonzo take care of the business, while he and Abbie took a well-deserved vacation. They visited Sacramento, Lake Tahoe, Carson City and Reno. Tom looked over the furniture stores in those places for ideas on the kinds of merchandise that were being offered for sale. They returned in September, well rested and with many new merchandising ideas.

On November 14, 1900, Tom Oakes received a telegram from his sister Jennie Chapman, who was then living in Angels Camp, California, She advised him that her husband Francis S. Chapman, then sixty-one, had died. Jennie asked Tom to advise their mother. The next morning Tom drove his horse and buggy to Willow Ranch and broke the sad news to Maggie.

While at the ranch, Tom again broached the subject of financing the furniture store building. He and Alonzo now held an option on the Main and Gay Street lot. Tom presented an estimate on the cost of erecting a brick building from C.E. Clough of Reno. Clough was constructing the new three-story Emerson Hotel building, and was also bidding on the new elementary school house. He had already set up his brickyard and kilns, and was baking bricks made from the clay found along the wash northeast of town.

After a family conference, the Greenos agreed to provide the funds needed, but as security took a mortgage on the building and property.

With financing assured, Tom and Alonzo completed the purchase of the lot on December 6, 1900. They asked for additional bids on the building, but Clough was the low bidder and they awarded him the contract.

April 24, 1901, turned out to be another exciting day at Willow Ranch. Kate, G Greeno's wife, gave birth to their first child, a girl whom they named Frances Maxine Greeno. This was the first grandchild for eighty-five-year-old George Greeno, and it made the old man very proud.

On Maggie's sixty-third birthday, Tom invited her to come to Susanville. Cap DeWitt, now fifteen, drove the horse and buggy. They celebrated her birthday by attending the grand opening and ball at the New Emerson Hotel on Monday, June 6, 1901. The occasion permitted Maggie to greet many of her Susanville friends. Everyone was greatly impressed with the new incandescent lights.

The following day, Tom and Alonzo gave Maggie and

Oakes and Philbrook building at Main and Gay Streets in Susanville, Lassen County, California (built 1901). Photo courtesy Lassen Historical Society, Susanville, California.

Cap an inspection tour of their new store. The building was soon to be completed, and the July 25, 1901, issue of the *Lassen Advocate* printed the following article:

> The Oakes and Philbrook building is approaching completion, it presents a decidedly neat appearance, fills out the vacant corner at Main and Gay Streets, and is a noticeable improvement to the appearance of our Main Street. The building has been wired for electric lights and when the interior is finished and stock in place, it will be a very attractive business place.

The August 1, *Lassen Advocate* carried the following amusing article about Tom Oakes.

We have a 'Good one' on T.A. Oakes, which
might easily been anything but a laughing matter. He spent Sunday out of town, and as a
means of amusement took with him a Marlin
'22' of which he is the possessor. Returning
home he removed, as he supposed, the diminu-
tive cartridges from his coat pocket. He didn't
get them all however, and Monday he loaded one
into his pipe with his tobacco, without noticing
it. Result: a shattered pipe, and startled furniture dealer. He is to be congratulated upon a
very fortunate escape from injury.

The cattle business continued to be quite profitable.
In September Senator Pat Flanigan, a prominent Ne-
vada stockman, came to Long Valley on a cattle-buying
mission. He purchased all the cattle H.L. Butters and
F.M. Rowland had for sale, and a large number from
Greeno and Clark.

The proceeds from the sale of beef received after the
fall rodeo provided sufficient profit for the Greenos and
Charlie Clark to pay off their mortgage to Jonathan
Roberts, as well as all their other financial obligations.
When "Uncle" George was informed that they were out
of debt, he admitted that he never expected to live long
enough to see the ranches clear of the debt they had
talked him into acquiring.

Maggie's eldest sons did not see eye to eye after
moving into their new furniture store building. In October they agreed to dissolve their partnership. Tom
Oakes sold his interest in the furniture store and undertaking business to Alonzo Philbrook. He retained
the planing mill and cabinet shop, and also title to the
heavily mortgaged new store building.

Tom Oakes upgraded his planing mill and shop. He

installed some new machinery that enabled him to make almost any item that could be made of wood.

During the early months of 1902, "Uncle" George Greeno suffering from the infirmities of old age, made several trips to see the doctor in Susanville. Maggie made every effort to comfort him, and accompanied him when one of the boys drove him into town.

Excitement was high again at Willow Ranch on August 22, 1902, when Emma Clark, gave birth to their second daughter, whom they named Catherine Irene Clark.

"Uncle" George Greeno was eighty-six in 1902, the year the newly organized Fair Association scheduled their first annual fair. His plan to attend was interrupted on Tuesday, September 16th, when he suffered a severe pain in his head. He was better the next day, but by Wednesday night he was stricken with apoplexy, and died peacefully after lapsing into unconsciousness. Both Maggie and his son G were with him until the end.

Alonzo Philbrook handled the funeral arrangements. The funeral was held at his Willow Ranch home on Friday, September 19th, at 2:00 P.M. His body was laid to rest in the cemetery on the ranch.

The *Lassen Advocate* of September 25, 1902, carried the following:

### CARD OF THANKS
We wish to express our gratitude to those who so kindly assisted us during the illness and after the death of our beloved husband and father.

Mrs. M.A. Greeno
G.W. Greeno

At Christmas dinner in 1902, the position at the head of the table, which until then had been occupied by the late patriarch George Greeno, was occupied by Maggie. All of her sons and their wives were together for the first time. In addition to Tom Oakes, Alonzo Philbrook, Charlie Clark, and G Greeno and their wives was her sixteen-year-old grandson, Cap DeWitt. Maggie's two-year-old granddaughter, Mary Estella, occupied a high chair at the table. Two infant granddaughters, Francis Maxine Greeno and Catherine Irene Clark, napped in a crib nearby.

During the meal, Tom Oakes advised the group that he had sold his planing mill and cabinet shop in Susanville, and they planned on moving to Reno. He and his brother-in-law, J.B. Nash, were negotiating to buy the Reno undertaking business of McPhail and Stewart.

The winter of 1903 was one of severe storms. Snow at times reached fifteen inches deep. Getting hay to the livestock kept Charlie, G, Cap, and Paiute Jack struggling under the severe conditions. Rains turned the snow to slush, the creeks rose and overflowed their banks. The wagons that replaced the sleighs buried themselves in the mud, and extra teams had to be attached to move the heavy loads of hay.

Tom Oakes and J.B. Nash completed the purchase of the McPhail and Stewart Reno undertaking business on February 5th. In order to make his portion of the payment for the business, Tom signed over his equity in the Susanville furniture store building. McPhail and Stewart then assumed the obligation for the balance due on the mortgage, on Tom's assurance that the rent paid by Philbrook would more than pay the debt.

By the following January, Alonzo Philbrook found himself in a bind financially with the furniture store: he was unable to pay the rent on the building, and his creditors were hounding him for money. Sheriff T.W. Wilson forced him into a bankruptcy merchandise sale.

McPhail and Stewart, not receiving rent money, threatened to sue Tom Oakes for misrepresentation and fraud. Clark and Greeno were not receiving any payments from McPhail and Stewart, and it appeared they would have to foreclose on the mortgage.

In the midst of the mortgage dispute, a baby boy was born at Willow Ranch on February 20, to Emma and Charlie Clark. They named their first son Charles Lawrence Clark.

When winter storms subsided and the roads dried enough to travel, Maggie, G, and Charlie went to Reno. With the assistance of an attorney they got Tom Oakes together with McPhail and Stewart. After much discussion, they finally worked out a settlement in which Clark and the Greenos agreed to pay McPhail and Stewart for their equity in the Susanville building. Clark and the Greenos acquired the full ownership of the building. McPhail and Stewart reassumed Oakes' interest in the Reno undertaking business, and the Oakes them moved to San Francisco.

Alonzo continued to operate the undertaking business in Susanville. He rented a building on upper Main Street, and started doing business for cash, selling wallpaper, lace curtains, window shades and miscellaneous household goods.

In the early fall Maggie, Charlie, and G consummated a deal with Fred Hines, President of the Bank of Lassen County, for the building they had repossessed. They accepted stock in the bank as payment, and Charles and G were elected to the bank's Board of Directors. Thereafter they made monthly trips to Susanville to attend the directors meetings.

In December, Maggie and her eighteen-year-old grandson Cap DeWitt went by train to San Francisco to visit Tom Oakes, and to enroll Cap in Healds Business School for the coming year.

# CHAPTER XVII

# DOYLE, THE RAILROAD TOWN

During the early 1900s, the Western Pacific Railroad Company made several surveys for a railroad from Salt Lake City, Utah, to the Pacific coast. After considering the various possible routes from Nevada through Lassen County to the Sacramento Valley, in 1905 they settled on a route along the eastern edge of Honey Lake Valley and through Long Valley, continuing down the Feather River Canyon. In early February 1905, E.H. Pew filed a map in the U.S. Land Office at Susanville, showing the right-of-way the railroad planned to acquire.

On their trip to attend the bank directors meeting, Charles and G called at the U.S. Land Office and viewed the railroad right-of-way map. They learned that the railroad would cross Willow Ranch, and the company would require a strip of their land 100 feet wide for three-quarters of a mile through their ranch meadow.

February 14, 1905, turned out to be another happy day for Maggie: a second grandson was born. Emma Clark gave birth to a boy they named him Edward Lyman Clark. Charlie told Maggie the baby was her valentine present. Thereafter, she always called him Eddie "Valentine" Clark.

Hot summer winds fanning wildfire flames on Sunday, August 25, threw Long Valley residents in a near-panic. The August 31 edition of the *Lassen Advocate* described the situation as follows:

DESTRUCTION OF FOREST FIRE

Last Sunday a fire was driven into Long Valley from the blazing forests by the strong winds prevailing that day, The residences of W.S. Robinson, and C.C. Ohl, were burned with all their contents the fire coming upon them so suddenly that no time was given for removing anything. The Willow Ranch property was seriously threatened as was also the Harlow place. From Mrs. Greeno's residence everything was removed. Little hope was entertained of saving any of these places, but fortunately change in direction of the wind, and devoted efforts of the people of the neighborhood averted a catastrophe. Quite a number went down from Milford, to lend their assistance in fighting the fire. From an eye witness it is learned that, whipped by the wind, the fire came down the wooded ridges almost as fast as a man could ride on horseback. While such occurrences are to be regretted in this instance there is grounds for rejoicing that the loss was not much greater.

Alonzo Philbrook sold his store and undertaking business to George L. Tombs on the first of November. One month later, he purchased from the estate of Gertrude Rose a wooden store building occupied by the Owl Saloon, on the north side of Main Street next to the I.O.O.F. building.

A tragedy struck at Willow Ranch on January 28, 1906. Two-year-old Charles Lawrence Clark was sitting on the floor playing with his little sister when he was suddenly afflicted. Within minutes death overtook him. The shock of the little boy's sudden death was overwhelming to his grandmother, Maggie, and to his parents. His funeral was held in the family home and burial was made in the Willow Ranch Cemetery.

Cap DeWitt finished his courses at Healds Business School the last of March. He left San Francisco for his return home on April 5, 1906. Waiting in Reno the next day to catch the NC&O train to Doyle, he learned that a great portion of San Francisco had been destroyed by an earthquake, and that fires were burning uncontrolled throughout the city. Maggie learned of the earthquake through a telegram received by the railroad station agent. She was greatly relieved when Cap stepped off the train at Doyle. She had not been certain that he had departed the city before the earthquake.

Surveying and grading work was in progress all along the Western Pacific route. Near the end of May 1907, the first spike was driven at the Salt Lake end of the route, heralding the assurance a transcontinental railroad would be operating through Long Valley, providing the farmers and stockmen direct access to the Bay Area and eastern United States markets.

Charlie and Emma were blessed with the arrival of a baby girl on October 6, 1907. They named Maggie's newest granddaughter Blanche Margaret Clark, in Maggie's honor.

That fall Alonzo repurchased the undertaking business he had sold to George L. Tombs the year before. The following week J.C. and George Long, operators of the Susanville-Reno stage, put a new "White Steamer" automobile into service, the first auto stage to operate through Long Valley on the Susanville-Reno route.

Cap DeWitt, at twenty-one, became infatuated with eighteen-year-old Lillian McKenzie, the daughter of Mrs. Sorenson, a resident of Standish in Honey Lake Valley. During the spring and summer of 1907, she accompanied him on numerous occasions to parties and dances in the area. They were married in Susanville on

September 14th. The ceremony was performed by County Judge F.A. Kelley. After the wedding the young couple took up residence on the Greeno ranch, moving into the Old Chamberlin Station ranch house.

That fall Charlie, G, and the other bank directors were faced with a serious problem and a great deal of worry, as a nationwide "hard coin" crisis engulfed the country. Many banks did not have sufficient coins available to cash checks. (Currency had not come into wide general use at that time. Gold and silver coins were the main monetary units.) Work on the Western Pacific tunnel at Beckwourth Pass was interrupted when storekeepers at Chilcoot refused to cash Western Pacific checks. The Bank of Lassen County, with prudent management, survived the crisis, but coins were very hard to procure for several months.

Maggie, at seventy, was honored with a surprise party on her birthday in June of 1908. Neighbor ladies gathered at her home for a pleasant afternoon of visiting, knitting, sewing, playing cards and enjoying the delicious refreshments served by Emma and Kate.

Construction work along the Western Pacific right-of-way created a demand for lumber to build construction camps. The Doyle and Crowder sawmill in Last Chance was busy cutting lumber: poles for pilings, railroad ties and bridge timbers. The timber products were hauled from the sawmill to the lumber yard near the railroad right-of-way, with a big 80 horsepower tractor engine.

Ranchers who had heavy wagons took jobs hauling materials out on the desert to the construction camps. Long Valley ranchers were hard pressed to provide the camps with fresh vegetables, and some contracted to butcher and deliver meat to the camps.

During all the railroad building excitement, Kate Greeno gave birth to a son they named Clemment. He was soon to be dubbed "Buster" by the family.

In late December, Cap DeWitt drove his wife Lillian, who was heavy with child, to Standish to spend the holidays with her mother. Lillian remained at Standish following the holidays, while Cap returned to his ranch chores in Long Valley.

Lillian gave birth to a baby girl on January 13, 1909. When Cap received the news that their first child had arrived, he rushed to Standish to be with his wife. They named the baby Edythe Louisa. A month later Cap returned to Standish and brought his wife and baby girl to their Long Valley home. Maggie, anxious to see her new great-granddaughter, was waiting at the DeWitt home when they arrived. She spent the rest of the day holding and coddling the baby, while Lillian got settled back in her home.

An unwelcome development that was to add considerably to the cost of beef production for Maggie and her boys took place in the spring of 1909. Congress established a forest reserve in Plumas and Lassen counties. Arthur Barrett was assigned as forest ranger to supervise the area. His arrival made it official that thereafter a permit would be required and a charge made for all livestock grazed on the forest reserve land.

Forest rangers, railroad surveyors and construction men contributed to a surge of social activities in the valley. The young unmarried girls on the ranches found the outsiders interesting and willing to socialize. They seized upon every opportunity to arrange parties and dances. On March 16th, Cap and Lillian DeWitt were the recipients of a surprise party by fourteen young friends. They enjoyed an evening playing games, dancing, playing cards and telling stories.

By midsummer, track crews had reached Long Valley. Emma Clark and Kate Greeno were both boarding teamsters engaged in hauling ties, pilings, and bridge timbers, to the crews working along the right-of-way.

Maggie received a letter from Tom Oakes informing her that his wife Abbie had given birth to a baby girl on August 25th. They named the baby Margaret, after her grandmother.

The Western Pacific crews drove the last spike in the first part of November at Spanish Creek in Plumas County, tying together the sections of railroad that had started in Salt Lake City, Utah, and Oakland, California, nearly three years before.

Maggie was one of the first Long Valley residents to ride the new Western Pacific passenger train from Doyle station to the Bay area. She went there to visit Tom and to get acquainted with her new granddaughter, Margaret. When she returned home in early 1910, she brought another canary.

Maggie had anticipated that once the railroad was built and in operation, things would revert to what had been the normal, quiet, rural life in the valley. That did not come about. The NC&O and the Western Pacific established a transfer point at Willow Ranch. Shipments from northeastern California and southeastern Oregon were transferred to the Western Pacific for east and west shipment. Freight, passengers and livestock arriving on the Western Pacific destined for northeastern California and southeastern Oregon were transferred to the NC&O. This activity required a number of freight handlers.

With the great number of livestock being transferred between railroads, the Western Pacific found they needed more room for corrals and storage. In March 1910, the Company purchased another strip of land adjacent to its right-of-way from Willow Ranch. Entrepreneurs began to harass Maggie and her boys to sell them property near the railroad upon which they could build store buildings and homes.

The transcontinental freight trains brought other

problems that Maggie had not anticipated. Hobos, riding the rails, left the trains when they stopped. The hungry wayfarers made their way to the nearest houses in search of a handout. The inhabitants of the Willow Ranch houses, a short distance from the tracks, were constantly pestered for meals. Maggie at first was inclined to help the wayfarers, but she soon found the request for handouts overwhelming. The hobos that offered to work for a meal she tried to accommodate; however, some hobos would sneak into the barn or sheds after dark and lay out their bedrolls. Charlie and G learned to check the barns and sheds each night and dislodge any men found, for fear they might set a fire while lighting their pipe tobacco.

In the middle of July, some of the hobos were pressed into assisting the ranchers and local residents in fighting a forest fire that threatened to burn field crops at Willow Ranch and other ranches along the foothills. The fire had been started by a careless sheepherder who allowed his camp fire to burn after he left camp. Maggie, thankful for their help, saw to it that each hobo who fought fire got a good square meal.

Maggie's brother Bill, known to the early settlers as "Uncle Billy West," passed away during the summer, after being hospitalized for several months suffering from the infirmities of old age and the rugged hardships endured by early pioneers. Maggie had Alonzo Philbrook bring Bill's body to long Valley for burial in the Willow Ranch Cemetery.

Another totally unexpected event happened on Monday night, September 4, 1910. At first it was thought to be an earthquake. A defective switch caused the locomotive and five freight cars to leave the track and overturn, scattering fruit and other freight in all directions. The engineer and fireman escaped serious injury, but rail traffic was held up for several days, until the wreckage could be cleared and the main line repaired. Maggie, along with everyone at Willow Ranch, rushed to the site of the overturned cars and locomotive to view the first major wreck to occur on the new Western Pacific Railroad line.

Maggie was in Richmond, California, with the Oakes family when another record snowfall struck Long Valley in January 1911. The cattle on the open range suffered from lack of food. Deep snow made it extremely difficult getting hay to the young stock in pasture and in the corrals. The long duration of heavy snow exhausted the supply of hay. Many ranchers were forced to ship in hay from Fallon, Nevada, Charlie and G were fortunate: their vast land holdings had provided them a sufficient supply.

By spring, the demand for property around the Western Pacific Depot had become so great that Maggie, Charlie and G began to consider subdividing a portion of Willow Ranch into a townsite. Maggie was not happy with the idea of cutting up the ranch property. However, encouraged by real estate men, J.C. Horn and W.H. Earl, they began the process of surveying and laying out the town of Doyle.

Following the spring rodeo, and after the cattle had been moved to the mountains for summer pasture, Charlie made a trip to Pacific Grove. While there he purchased the first automobile to be owned by the Willow Ranch, a fine new 40 horsepower Buick touring car which he drove home. Not to be outdone by his older half-brother, G Greeno bought a new Dorris automobile. The Willow Ranch proprietors had now moved their personal transportation methods into the mechanical age.

The ground moisture resulting from the heavy winter storms brought on an extra-heavy hay crop in the valley. Willow Ranch crops in 1911 exceeded those of previous years, even though the new subdivision and the railroad right-of-way had eliminated several acres of hay land.

All hands were busy getting in the second hay crop when Abbie Oakes and her year-old daughter Margaret arrived on the Western Pacific from Richmond. They spent several days at Willow Ranch visiting Maggie; then Charlie drove them to Susanville in his new Buick. Abbie spent several more days there, visiting with her former acquaintances.

By fall, several buildings had been erected in the new town. The Phillips Hotel Company completed a hotel near the depot. Herbert F. Smart erected a one-story store building, and the Constantia Mercantile Company opened a small store.

G Greeno was called to serve on the Lassen County Grand Jury in January 1912. While in Susanville, he was approached by Sheriff A.C. Hunsinger to serve as a deputy sheriff in the fast-growing Doyle area. On her return from Richmond, where she had spent the winter, Maggie was quite disturbed to learn G had been deputized. She feared he might become embroiled in a shootout with some of the unsavory characters that got off the trains at Doyle, or an occasional cattle rustler he might be called upon to arrest.

Maggie found it hard to comprehend all the changes that were taking place on her ranch, with all the building in the town of Doyle. The rapid urbanization of the rural area had not been planned, and was totally unexpected.

A restaurant opened in a new building that had just been completed by W.H. Earl, who was the sales agent for the new townsite. The Phillips Hotel added eight more rooms, two baths, a reception room and a ladies entrance. The Doyle Land and Hotel Company announced plans to build a two-story store and office

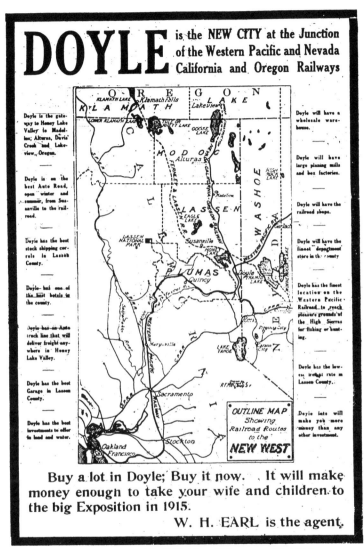

Advertisement in *Lassen Mail*, Friday, February 23, 1912.

building. Mr. A. Wiles purchased several lots and erected a store building and a cottage. A community amusement hall was erected during the summer, and it was well used for business and social events. Pyramid

Lake Indians found a ready market among the Doyle people for the large Pyramid Lake trout they brought by wagon loads and peddled about the town. Western Pacific crews were busy constructing another side track, and enlarging the livestock corrals to handle the large influx of livestock being transferred between railroads. The increasing number of passengers arriving and departing on the Western Pacific trains caused Joslyn and Holmes to put on a second daily auto-stage from Susanville.

All was not always peace and quiet in the little town. The residents had just about become accustomed to the rattle and whistle of the trains day and night, the chugging auto-stages, and the daily trips of the tractor with its squeaking wagons of lumber, when a loud explosion woke the entire population at 12.30 A.M. August 13, 1912. A tractor loaded on a flatcar at the Western Pacific unloading platform exploded. It scattered parts over a wide area. Residents rushed to the scene, some still in their night jackets, to determine the cause of their rude awakening.

On February 2nd, 1913, following a Saturday night dance, a defective flue set fire to the new Doyle Hall. Lacking fire-fighting equipment, the people could only watch and work to prevent the flames from spreading. The new hall and all its contents burned to the ground.

A group of Doyle women gathered in late February and organized the Doyle Improvement Club. Their first project was to raise money to rebuild the town hall. Emma Clark was elected president, and Kate Greeno treasurer. When Maggie returned from her winter sojourn at Richmond and learned about the loss of the community hall, she readily raised the amount of the contribution Willow Ranch had pledged to the hall fund.

On Saturday, March 1, the club sponsored a public

chicken dinner at which they served 108 people. Emma and Kate were on the committee and helped to prepare the dinner.

In order to have a meeting place and entertainment center until a new hall could be financed and built, W.S. Thompson procured a large tent, in which social activities were held.

On Sunday June 1, the Ladies Improvement Club held a reception in the tent to honor Maggie's seventy-fifth birthday. The ladies invited the public to attend and pay their respects to the matriarch of Willow Ranch. Maggie's Yankee ingenuity, tenacity, perseverance and hard work, had inspired her late husband and her sons to build a ranching and livestock business, from 160 acres and a small herd of scrawny range cattle into a vast land holding and a large herd of prime beef cattle. Friends, relatives and acquaintances old and new dropped by to wish Maggie many more years of health and happiness. many of those that attended the reception volunteered pledges to help rebuild the town hall.

Butler and Hughes had placed in service the first auto-truck to operate hauling freight between Doyle and Susanville. On June 30 the auto-truck, loaded with hay, caught on fire and burned. Many of the old-time stockmen were convinced the fire proved that auto-trucks could never replace the horse and mule teams.

Doyle held its first Fourth of July celebration that year. The main feature of the day was a baseball game between the ranch boys and the town and railroad boys. Local Indians entertained in the tent with native dances. Molly and Paiute Jack were active participants. The Ladies Club sold cookies and lemonade to raise money for the hall fund.

On August 29, 1913, Lillian, Cap DeWitt's wife, gave birth to their second child, a girl they named Barbara Elenora. Mrs. Olds, a neighbor lady and practicing midwife, attended Lillian until Dr. Molton arrived and delivered the baby. Maggie sent Molly to the DeWitt home to help with the housework and assist in the care of four-year-old Edythe until Lillian was able to resume her household chores.

A community Christmas tree, sponsored by the Sunday school, was held in the tent. The program was presided over by Mr. J.S. Dixon, the owner of the new hardware and furniture store, who was also the Sunday school teacher. A quartet of male and female voices and recitations and readings by the children provided the entertainment. Santa Claus, parents and friends attended, including Maggie, the Clark's and their children.

On December 28, G Greeno returned from Reno, where he had gone with his wife and children to spend Christmas with Kate's parents. He complained of a cold in his chest and problems breathing. Within a couple of days he was confined to his bed. Maggie delayed her planned trip to Richmond in order to assist in his care. Dr. Garner was summoned from Susanville, and determined that G had contracted pneumonia and required round-the-clock care. Charlie telegraphed Kate to come from Reno at once, and to bring two nurses to attend G. Kate arrived at their Willow Ranch home at 3:15 A.M. the next morning with the nurses. They did everything in the way of medical assistance to improve his condition. Dr. Garner remained with him constantly for three days and nights, but was unable to check the malady.

George W. "G" Greeno Jr. died on Sunday January 4, 1914, at the age of forty-one. His wife Kate, was unwilling to bury him in the Willow Ranch cemetery, she insisted that his half-brother Alonzo Philbrook arrange for a funeral and burial in Susanville. His funeral ser-

Town of Doyle, Long Valley, Lassen County, California (c. 1915). Photo from an old postcard, courtesty Lassen Historical Society, Susanville, California.

vice was held on January 6, at the Susanville Methodist church. Master Stanley Tyler of the Janesville Masonic lodge conducted the service, and Reverend J.P. Westervelt delivered the eulogy. In attendance were many loyal friends and neighbors, some coming all the way from Reno over exceedingly troublesome dirt winter roads.

The sudden death of her youngest son was almost more than Maggie's frail body could endure. She decided to spend the winter on the ranch, taking a couple of short jaunts to Carson City, Nevada, to visit her daughter Jennie Chapman, and to seek medical attention in Reno.

By March, Doyle was beginning to appear more like a small town instead of an unorganized group of shacks. The streets were being graded and trees were planted along them. Although the residents did not recognize the fact, the town had already passed the apex of its boom.

The Southern Pacific Railroad had completed a branch line from Fernley, Nevada, through Honey Lake Valley into the timberlands twenty miles west of Susanville, to transport lumber from the Red River Lumber Company's mill. The Southern Pacific and the NC&O tracks crossed at Amedee, and that became the active transfer point for freight consigned to northeastern California and southeastern Oregon. Susanville and Honey Lake Valley residents found the Southern Pacific more convenient for their travel in and out of the area.

Activities at Doyle station began to falter. Fewer railroad workers and stage passengers used the Doyle

Four generations (c. 1900s). Left to right Maggie, great-granddaughter Marcile Richardson, granddaughter Margaret (Chapman) Richardson, daughter Jane "Jennie" (Oakes) Chapman. Photo courtesy Jay Richardson.

Hotel, or patronized the town's business establishments.

The death of G Greeno brought many changes at Willow Ranch. The burden of operating the vast livestock operation and ranch lands fell upon the broad shoulders of Charlie Clark. Maggie, although suffering from the infirmities of age, endeavored to keep abreast of the ranch business. Kate Greeno had taken up residence in Reno during the school year, where her children Maxine and Clemment were enrolled. She returned to her Willow Ranch home only during the school vacations, and was not always readily available to participate in the day-to-day decisions required in the vast operation.

Maggie often accompanied Charlie to Susanville when he went to attend the bank directors meetings. She used the occasions to shop, visit friends, and consult with Dr. Garner about her ailments. In May, she consulted her lawyer regarding her will and other legal affairs.

On June 3rd, the four Clark and two Greeno children staged an impromptu party for their grandmother on her seventy-sixth birthday, serving her and themselves with cake that had been prepared by Emma. Maggie also received the usual birthday messages from her three older children.

During 1915, war was raging in Europe. The demand for grain and meat had all the ranchers in the United States striving to increase production. Maggie urged Charlie to plant every spare acre into grain, and to withhold every fertile cow from market in order to increase their calf crop.

Early in January, W.O. McDevitt came to the valley on a horse-buying mission for the French Army. He offered to pay $75.00 for cavalry horses, and $105.00 for Artillery horses. Unfortunately Willow Ranch had only a few horses that they could spare.

In May, Cap DeWitt who had been farming the old Chamberlin Station ranch on a lease from the Greeno estate, reached an agreement with Kate Greeno and Charlie Clark to purchase that ranch.

Maggie accompanied Charlie to Susanville in August to see her doctor about the pain she had been experiencing. Dr. Garner suggested she remain in town for a few days so he could provide her with daily treatments. She stayed with her long-time friend Mrs. W.H. Earl for two weeks while undergoing treatments. During the rest of 1915, Maggie accompanied Charlie to Susanville once a month for further medical attention.

Severe blizzards ushered in 1916. Temperatures stood at zero with winds gusting to 60 miles, blowing snow. in order for Charlie to get to Susanville on January 4, he had to cross the desert to Amedee by team. Leaving his horses there, he rode the Southern Pacific train to Susanville.

On the morning following his return to the ranch he learned that an itinerant named Thomas Prior had stolen one of his best saddle horses. He immediately notified Sheriff Hunsinger.

The thief had started for Nevada but lost his way during the night, ending up in Byrd Flat the next morning. After a rancher there recognized Charlie's horse, Prior turned the horse loose and took to the hills on foot. His footprints in the snow were easily followed over the rough terrain, and the sheriff caught up with and arrested him without a struggle.

During the storm, Maggie's son, Coroner Philbrook, had been called to Grasshopper Valley to conduct an inquest into the death of two men, who had burned to death at the Gerig Ranch. The storm was so severe that Alonzo was unable to return for a week. Susanville residents were quite concerned for his safety. Maggie, not being advised of his absence, was spared the worry it would have otherwise caused her. Charlie Clark caused her enough distress on his trip to Susanville. He had to go around by Standish, as the road from Janesville was impassable. The storm delayed his return for several days.

On Charlie's March trip to the bank directors meeting, Maggie accompanied him. She spent several extra days in Susanville, undergoing medical treatment. On her return to the ranch, Maggie, in her pride, reported that her health was much improved. However, it was apparent to all that she was suffering.

On October 29, Cap and Lillian became the proud parents of a great-grandson for Maggie. They named the boy Charles Arthur DeWitt after his father and grandfather. As Maggie was no longer able to get about without great effort and suffering, when Lillian was able to ride they took, the new baby to Willow Ranch for her to see.

A month later, the pain in Maggie's frail, bedridden body was eased only by the suppressants prescribed by her sympathetic doctor. In fleeting moments of semi-consciousness, the happy events and the many sorrows she had experienced during her life passed in review through her mind. The journey through life that began in Boston in 1838 drew to a close. On December 5, 1916, after seventy-eight years, six months and two days, the matriarch cattle queen of Long Valley, Margaret Ann (Wallace) Greeno, closed her eyes for the last time as her spirit departed the tired body.

Her funeral was held the next day at her Willow Ranch home under the direction of her son, Alonzo Kelly Philbrook. The Reverend Mr. J.H. Westervelt of the Susanville Methodist church conducted the service attended by her family, neighbors, acquaintances of many years, and her faithful Indian servants, Molly and Paiute Jack. Her body was laid to rest in the Willow Ranch Cemetery at Doyle, between her brother William West, and her husband of thirty-one years, George W. Greeno.

# ACKNOWLEDGEMENTS

This narrative is a synthesis of information gathered from many sources and many persons. Space does not permit a listing of all the kind and helpful people in libraries, county and state offices throught northern California, and universities from Boston, Massachusetts, to San Francisco and Chico, California, who assisted in the research of historical documents and records. However, those persons that went beyond the bounds of courtesy and read the manuscript or portions thereof, made suggestions, or helped in other ways deserve to be acknowledged.

The late Katherine I. Clark, and Blanche M. Clark, granddaughters of Maggie Greene, for their personal recollections, photos from their family album, excerpts from the Greeno family Bible and reviewing the first draft of the manuscript.

Mr. Jay Richardson, great-grandson of Maggie Greene, for photos and his recollections of his family's memories of Maggie.

My wife Barbara DeWitt McDow, great-granddaughter of Maggie, for her recollections of family stories about Maggie, and for her assistance in reviewing and checking the several drafts of the manuscript.

Mr. Phillip S. Hall, retired rancher and native of Long Valley, for the abundant historical information he provided on Long Valley ranches.

Mr. Tim I. Purdy, Lassen County Historian, for his assistance researching Lassen County historical events.

Mr. John H. Nopel, retired educator and Butte County Historian, reviewing the Butte County segment of the manuscript.

Mrs. Mildred Forester, Historian of the Paradise Ridge Communities, for her assistance and information on Inskip, the Chaparral House and photos.

Edna K. DeWitt, great-granddaughter-in-law of Maggie Greeno, great help in reviewing and rewriting the various manuscript drafts.

Elizabeth N. Metzger, for her valuable assistance in editing the manuscript.

GEORGE McDOW, JR.

George McDow, Jr., a native Californian, was raised in the historic community of Susanville, Lassen County, California, situated on the Old Noble Immigrant Trail.

Fascinated by the tales told by pioneer settlers, to their offspring of experiences encountered in early-day mining camps and on western stock ranches, he developed an insatiable curiosity to research and record that pervading spirit and the achievements of those who contributed so much to the development of northeastern California.

After 35 years employed in the lumber industry he retired and moved to Chico, Butte County, California, where he has pursued his interest in historical research. Seeking out the accomplishments of pioneers, and the women who had been ignored by a male-dominated society. He has contributed many historical stories through talks, and written articles for historical societies, and authored the book *Booms and Mushrooms*, a story of Susanville from 1910 to 1930, published by Lahontan Images, Susanville, California.

# Bibliography

**Biographies**

Abbott, Joshua A. — Fariss and Smith, *History of Plumas, Lassen and Sierra Counties*, 1882, p. 294.

Carter, Dr. J.S. — *History of Plumas, Lassen and Sierra Counties, 1882*, p. 307 and *The Sierras* by J.M. Guinn, Chapman Publ. Co. Chicago, 1906, p. 726.

Chamberlin, Rueben — Faris and Smith, *History of Plumas, Lassen and Sierra Counties*, 1882, p. 403.

Clark, Charles B. — *The Sierras* by J.M. Guinn, Chapman Publ. Co. Chicago, 1906, p. 460.

Greeno, George — Fariss and Smith, *History of Plumas, Lassen and Sierra Counties,* 1882, p. 406.

Greeno, George W. — *The Sierras* by J.M. Guinn, Chapman Publ. Co. Chicago, 1906, p. 629.

Greeno, Mrs. M.A. — *The Sierras* by J.M. Guinn, Chapman Publ. Co. Chicago, 1906, p. 457.

Long, Wm. B. — Fariss and Smith, *History of Plumas, Lassen and Sierra Counties*, 1882, p. 409.

Olsen, Peter — *The Sierras* by J.M. Guinn, Chapman Publ. Co. Chicago, 1906, p. 739.

Philbrook, Alonzo K. — *The Sierras* by J.M. Guinn, Chapman Publ. Co. Chicago, 1906, p. 401.

Roop, Isaac Newton — Fariss and Smith, *History of Plumas, Lassen and Sierra Counties*, 1882, p. 412 and *The Sierras* by J.M. Guinn, Chapman Publ. Co. Chicago, 1906, p. 335.

Steinberger, J.M. — Fariss and Smith, *History of Plumas, Lassen and Sierra Counties*, 1882, p. 500.

Stover, Reuben — Fariss and Smith, *History of Plumas, Lassen and Sierra Counties*, 1882, p. 322, and *The Sierras* by J.M. Guinn, Chapman Publ. Co. Chicago, 1906, p. 670.

Stover, Thaddeus S. — *The Sierras* by J.M. Guinn, Chapman Publ. Co. Chicago, 1906, p. 721.

Wood, General Allen — Fariss and Smith, *History of Plumas, Lassen and Sierra Counties*, 1882, p. 197.

**Books**

Alley, B.F. — *History of Tuolumne County,* 1882.

Barthold, Victor M., Ph.D. — *The Pacific Steamer California*, Houghton-Mifflin Co., Boston, Ma.

Buchsman, Lamont — *Ships of Steam*. McGraw-Hill Book Co. Inc. 1956.

Dudde, Erwin G. — *California Gold Camps*. INSKIP. University of California Press, Berkeley, 1975.

DeNevi, Donald F. — *Western Pacific Railroad*. Seattle Supervisor, 1978.

Fairfield, A.M. — *Pioneer History of Lassen County*, Chapman and Co. San Francisco, 1916.

Gould, Chas. & David Staples — *The Boston-Newton Co.*, Lincoln University of Nebraska Press, 1969.

Lindsey, Donald Barr, — *Panama Canal*, Crown Publishers Inc. N.Y., 1970.

Mansfield, George C.    *History of Butte County*, Los Angeles Historic Record Co., 1908.

McCullough, David    *Paths Between the Seas*, Simon and Schuster N.Y., 1977.

McGie, Joseph F.    *History of Butte County,* Butte County Board of Education, 1956–1982.

Myrick, David F.    *Railroads of Nevada*, Howell-North, Berkely, 1962-1963.

Nadeau, Remi    *Ghost Towns and Mining Camps of California*, The Ward-Rithe Press, Los Angeles, 1965.

New England Economic Research Foundation    *New England Railroads*. Boston, Massachusetts, 1965.

Pacific Mail Steamship Co.    *Pacific Mail Steamship Co., and United States Mail and Steamship Co.*, Boston, Ma.

Seaburg, Carl    *History of Boston*, Boston Beacon Press, Boston, Ma., 1971.

Talbitzar, Bill    *Butte County*, Windsor Publications, 1987.

Thompson and West    *History of Sutter County*, reproduced by Howell-North, 1974.

Wells, Harry L. & W.L. Chambers,    *History of Butte County*, 1892, reproduced by Howell-North Books, 1973.

Weston, Otheto    *Mother Lode Album*, Stanford University Press, 1948.

**Newspapers**

*Alta California Daily*    Microfilm viewed at San Francisco Main Library. 1858 and 1859.

*Lassen Sage Brush*    Microfilm viewed at California State University, Chico. 1864 thru 1868.

*Lassen Advocate*    Microfilm viewed at California State University, Chico. 1868 thru 1916.

*Lassen Mail*    Microfilm viewed at California State University, Chico. 1912 thru 1916.

*The Union Democrat 1849-1949 Centennial Edition*    Viewed at Tuolumne County Library, Sornora, Ca.

**Historical Society Publications**

Butte County Historical Society    *Diggins*, Vol. 1 thru Vol. 35, viewed at Chico Branch, Butte County Library, Chico, Ca.

Paradise Historical Society    *Tales of Paradise Ridge*, Vol. 1 thru Vol. 28, viewed at Chico Branch, Butte County Library, Chico, Ca.

**Unpublished Articles**

Hall, Phillip S.    *Constantia*, History of s small town in Lassen County, Ca. Lassen College, Susanville, Ca., 1985.

Coates, Frank C.    *Early History of Tuolumne County*. Reviewed at Tuolumne County Library, Sonora, Ca.

**Public Records**

VIEWED AT MASSACHUSETTS ARCHIVES, Columbia Point, 220 Morresy Rd., Boston, Ma.

*New Journal of Commerce*. Spring Edition, 1849.

United States Census Microfilm, 1840 and 1850.

Massachussets State Census Microfilm, 1845 and 1855.

Records of ships sailing from Boston, 1850 thru 1858.

Marriage records, 1841 thru 1857.

Voters registration, 1840 thru 1858.

VIEWED AT NEW ENGLAND GENEALOGICAL SOCIETY, 101 Newbury St., Boston, Ma.

Boston City Directories, 1849 thru 1858.

VIEWED AT SPECIAL COLLECTIONS DEPARTMENT, MERIAM LIBRARY, CALIFORNIA STATE UNIVERSITY, CHICO, Ca.

Butte County Voter Registrations, 1860 thru 1864.

Butte County Assessor's Records, 1857 thru 1864.

Butte County Marriage Records, 1860 thru 1864.

Microfilm: United States Census, Butte County, Ca., 1860 thru 1870.

Microfilm: United States Census, Lassen County, Ca., 1870 thru 1910.

Microfilm: United States Census, Santa Clara County, Ca., 1970.

VIEWED AT LASSEN COUNTY RECORDER'S OFFICE, COURT HOUSE, Susanville, Ca.

Deeds and early records, 1864 thru 1916.

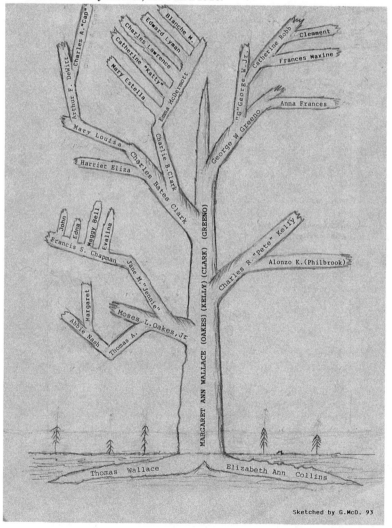

Sketched by G.McD. 93